the CURRENCY
of LIFE

the CURRENCY *of* LIFE

Uncovering the Clues to Why We're Here

MARK E. KLEIN, M.D.

Greenbriar Publishing, LLC
Potomac, Maryland

Manufactured in the United States of America

Publisher's Cataloging-in-Publication
(Provided by Quality Books, Inc.)

Klein, Mark E.
    The currency of life : uncovering the clues to why we're here / Mark E. Klein.
        p. cm.
    Includes index.
    LCCN 2010906281
    ISBN-13: 978-0-9761684-1-6
    ISBN-10: 0-9761684-1-3

    1. Religious life. 2. Meaning (Philosophy)
I. Title.

BL624.K54 2010   204
                      QBI10-600102

Designed by Janice Benight

DEDICATION

To my family—all six billion of you

ACKNOWLEDGMENTS

Many thanks to:

My editor, Justin Misik.

My designer, Janice Benight.

My friend, Dr. Todd Johns.

And especially to the love of my life, my wife Deneen.

Each of you knows how much I appreciate
your assistance in creating this book.

Contents

Acknowledgments *vii*

PART I   THE WORLD IS NOT WHAT YOU THINK *1*

a story   *Separate Lives* *3*

chapter 1   Contemplation *11*

chapter 2   Framing the Issue *19*

chapter 3   The Approach *27*

chapter 4   The Hard Clues—Relativity *37*

chapter 5   The Hard Clues—The Quantum World *51*

chapter 6   The Softer Clues *63*

chapter 7   Reality *77*

chapter 8   History *87*

a story   *A Tale of Two Families* *97*

chapter 9   Man Plans God Laughs *107*

chapter 10   Common Threads *121*

PART II   WHAT THE WORLD IS *129*

chapter 11   There Is No Pie *131*

chapter 12   The Currency of Life *141*

chapter 13   Family *151*

chapter 14   Violence *161*

chapter 15   Nothing But Now *169*

a story   *The Dreams* *177*

chapter 16   Perfection *189*

Index *207*

PART I

THE WORLD IS NOT WHAT YOU THINK

Separate Lives

"Robert," Dr. Benjamin asked me on one of my first days as his associate, "what would you say if a neighbor rang your doorbell at three a.m. one night and asked for your help with her sick husband?"

Before I could answer, Dr. Benjamin provided the response.

"You would say thank you, Robert, that's what you would say. You would say thank you because your neighbor, by ringing your doorbell, is telling you that she trusts you with the life of one of her most precious possessions. You thank her, and then you thank God for this great honor He has bestowed upon you, and while you're talking to the good Lord you pray that you don't screw up and make her husband worse."

At the conclusion of almost every paragraph, there was the humor. Dr. Benjamin reminded me daily that although we were blessed to do this work, to enjoy the trust of our patients, we must never take ourselves too seriously. We were men with important responsibilities, nothing more, and that made us anything but unique.

"Let me tell you a little story, Robert."

When I heard those words I became mesmerized, like a child on his father's lap before bedtime. There was no such thing as a "little story" from Dr. Benjamin's lips. He was Aesop; something important was about to be revealed, and I was afraid that if I missed even one of his fables, I would be in danger of falling victim to some otherwise avoidable disaster at some future moment in my life. Sometimes the lesson was about the art of medicine; more often it was a metaphor for life. And God knows I needed as much help as I could get in that area.

My own father died when I was twenty-one. I first learned of his illness when I retuned home from college for Thanksgiving of my senior year. I was carrying my suitcases to my bedroom when I heard my mother enter the room.

"Hi Mom," I began, embracing her and bending down to kiss her right cheek. My mother was a tiny woman, barely five feet tall with heels. I noticed a peculiar smile on her face as she said, "I have something to talk with you about."

For some reason I anticipated good news, that our family would be taking a trip over that Christmas break, something we had never done together. I don't know why that was the thought that filled my mind at that moment; perhaps it was that strange smile that told me something was different. What I heard next from my mother—her tiny body I suddenly noticed now slightly trembling—was a far cry from my hopeful expectation.

"Daddy is sick. He has cancer."

Those words marked the beginning of the end of my childhood, which would come to a screeching halt eighteen months later with my father's death and my mother's sale of my childhood home and relocation to another state. I sorely missed those years of young adulthood with my father, when the bravado of adolescence has faded and the thirst for real life knowledge begins. For a young man, a father usually fills the role of guide and teacher. Perhaps he would have had no words of wisdom for me. Perhaps he would have left me to fend for myself, and perhaps I would have made all of the same mistakes I committed in his absence. But how could I know? We don't get a chance to "try on" life with one set of experiences and then try another, like two sizes of trousers, and see which fits the best. The loss of my father meant the beginning of a great deal of trial-and-error learning on my part, and unfortunately more of the latter than former.

Until, that is, I met Dr. Jim Benjamin. Dr. Benjamin never meant to be my surrogate father, but then again he never meant to be anyone's father, spiritual leader, or confessor. Or to play any of so many other roles pressed on him by family, friends, colleagues, and patients. I was but one of many people with whom he shared his time and wisdom, I knew, but I treasured each day with him and kept my ears open for a sign that another lesson was on its way. And when he said those words—let me tell you a little story, Robert—it was time to stop whatever I was doing and pay attention.

■ ■ ■

Philip often found himself wrestling with a repetitive thought. It could be while dining with his university colleagues on a nothing-special mid-winter evening, or while alone in a bar, hovering over a warm beer. Whenever and wherever, Philip was so often immersed in that sadly familiar thought. "It wasn't supposed to be this way," he reflected. Life, specifically his life, was not supposed to be what it had turned out to be. The woman he had just left at home with his children, his wife, was the wrong one. His job was supposed to be someone else's, and someone else's job his. He was living in the wrong house in the wrong neighborhood, heard the wrong sounds when he spoke, and saw the wrong face staring back at him from the mirror. Some parts of all of it, and all parts of some of it, were wrong. In times past his eyes would swell with tears. It was far too familiar for that now. These days when Philip was immersed in that reverie, he just stared straight ahead and tried as best as he could to bear the weight pressing his shoulders towards the floor.

Late one fall afternoon Joshua entered the laboratory he shared with Philip and saw his friend with his head in his hands, his shoulders drooping low, not a muscle in motion. Of late this was a recurring theme, and the Nobel-nominated physicist grew saddened as he once again witnessed his friend and colleague in an obvious state of melancholy. This time, however, he was certain he would lift his friend's spirits.

"Philip!" Joshua said.

Philip raised his head, more slowly than one would have imagined given the decibel level of Joshua's address. He did not respond; he just looked in Joshua's direction.

"I finished the calculation you suggested. No asymmetries, not a one. We have found it, my friend."

Philip smiled, slowly rose from his chair, embraced his best friend, and laid his head on Joshua's shoulder.

"I know, Philip. I know how difficult this has been for you. But I think we might actually be able to make it better very soon."

Depression was not Philip's problem, as Joshua had understood now for over a year. When he first met Philip three years ago, he had assumed that this quiet, secretive physicist was just another academically brilliant but socially inept scientist. After all, there were so many like him—who would have really noticed the subtle signs? Only after almost two years working side by side with Philip did Joshua begin to appreciate the significance of those signs. Philip didn't avoid eye contact, or wear mismatched clothing as if he dressed in the dark, or exhibit any of the other clichéd attributes of the mad scientist. He was always impeccably groomed and unfailingly polite. He just said very little—his answers to questions were like the abbreviated text messages Joshua's teenagers substituted for real human conversation. Though married with children, Philip never attended the department's social functions, nor did he accept invitations for his family to share a Sunday afternoon with his colleagues and their families.

"It will be a risk, my friend. I really have no idea what's going to happen. You'll have to share it with Lauren. Do you want me to explain it to her?"

Lauren, Philip's wife, was simply a lovely woman. She radiated kindness and intelligence. Joshua had grown very fond of Lauren and the family's two small daughters. In fact, it was Lauren who had initially begged Joshua to intervene. The past few years of their marriage had been lonely and sad for both. Probably only because they were both such wonderful human beings were their girls spared the heartache that so commonly results when parents are psychologically separated by a great distance.

"I'll tell her, Josh. But I think it would help if you were there. How long until we can attempt the transfer?"

"Anytime. It will either work or not; I honestly have no idea. It's completely up to you if you want to go for it."

"I'm ready," Philip said. "I don't want to wait; it will only get harder for everyone. Tonight?"

"What time will the girls be in bed?"

"Seven-thirty."

"I'll be over then." Philip embraced Joshua again. As he let his friend go, he sighed and fixed him with a warm but sad smile. "Thank you, Josh. Whatever, you know..."

"I know, my friend. You don't have to say anymore. I know."

■ ■ ■

At 7:30 that evening Lauren tucked in Melissa, at five the younger of the two girls. At the same moment, Philip turned off the overhead light as he exited Marguerite's room. Lauren turned and saw Philip in the doorway.

"Let's go downstairs," she whispered to Philip. "I heard what you said to Marguerite. I don't understand. What did you mean by that?" she inquired of her husband as they reached the kitchen.

Before Philip could answer they noticed Joshua seated at the table.

"Joshua, I didn't know you were coming over," Lauren began as she approached her husband's closest friend. Lauren shot a glance back at Philip who was just behind her, her eyes clearly indicating she knew something was going on between the two men. She returned to Josh, gave him a slight embrace, and touched her cheek to his.

All three fell silent. Joshua and Lauren instinctively turned to Philip.

"Right, it's my turn." Philip looked at Joshua. "I haven't yet told her what we are planning to try..."

"Try? Try what?" Lauren interrupted.

Philip pulled out a kitchen chair for Lauren.

"Lauren, I need you to sit. I have a lot to tell you."

"Then you've decided to leave me. It's true, isn't it?" Lauren looked straight at Joshua. "Tell me I'm wrong."

Joshua said nothing.

"I'm not wrong." She turned back towards Philip. "You're leaving." Lauren began to cry.

"Lauren, you must hear me. Yes, I am leaving, but I should never even have been here. Three years ago you told me you noticed I was different, that I wasn't the same Philip you had married. You were right, Lauren, I wasn't. But it wasn't like you think. I didn't suddenly change. I mean I have always been this way, even though to you I suddenly seemed like a stranger, literally overnight."

Philip's demeanor changed. His head dropped just a bit, and his eyes began to moisten.

"What I am about to tell you is so ... so unimaginable, I'm afraid you will think me mad. I'm not crazy, or depressed." He paused to take a breath. "That's why Joshua is here. He knows everything I am about to tell you, and I know you trust him.

You went to sleep one night, secure and very much in love with your Philip beside you, and awoke in the morning beside someone who I am sure must have seemed a total stranger. Your Philip looked exactly the same as he had only hours earlier, but something about him was so foreign.

I am that stranger next to whom you awoke that morning, not the Philip you had kissed goodnight before drifting off to sleep. I look the same as that Philip, but we are otherwise so very different. You know you would never have married Philip if he—if I—were always like this, like I have been for the past three years. You've just about told me that a hundred times, and you were right. I'm not that Philip."

Josh interceded. "Lauren, let me help. This man's name is Philip Merrin. He was born on June 12, 1972. His parents are Marshall and Lorna Merrin. All that you know. But this Philip Merrin is not the one you married. Remember that lecture I gave last summer on parallel universes? It's not fiction, Lauren. Physicists like me and Philip have long postulated the existence of these parallel universes. This Philip Merrin is from another universe, a universe exactly like ours, one that invisibly exists right alongside ours, only the stories in that universe are different. This Philip Merrin didn't marry Lauren Goodson. He didn't have two beautiful girls. He's a physicist like your husband Philip, but it probably would have been better if he wasn't."

Philip continued. "I was working on black holes. In my lab we worked with ultra-dense matter. Until I confided in Joshua last year and he heard my plight, no one in this universe had realized how easy it is to create this material in a particle collider. Imagine creating the equivalent of a black hole in a room the size of this kitchen. That's what I did one evening three years ago. I was unprepared for the effect of my successful experiment, and before I had any idea what was occurring I was swept into the blackness. In what was essentially frozen time, your Philip and I were exchanged. Neither of us missed a single heartbeat.

I know, it's beyond bizarre. But Lauren, you've known for some time, maybe even from the night I arrived, that your husband was different."

Lauren didn't move or utter a sound as Philip concluded his story. For a minute or two she just stared straight ahead, unemotionally digesting what she had just heard. When she had finished whatever processing she had needed to do, still looking at no one in particular, she quietly asked, "Can we get him back?"

She then turned towards the man named Philip whom until just a few minutes ago she had assumed was her husband.

"Can we get *my* Philip back?" Her sad eyes seemed to beg for it.

Philip didn't answer. Lauren turned away from him.

"Josh?"

"I don't know, Lauren. Maybe, yes. I think it's possible. We'll just have to see."

"When will we know? Philip, you said you were leaving. So that's what you meant? You are going to try? The two of you are going to try to send you back?"

"That's the plan, Lauren. We're going to try tonight. Now."

Lauren began to sob, first just a little and soon uncontrollably. Philip kneeled and took her hands.

"I feel so responsible. I had no idea this could even happen. I miss my family terribly, but my longing for them doesn't begin to match my heartache over what you and the girls have lost. I am so, so sorry Lauren."

Lauren looked away, now expressionless. Phillip squeezed her hands.

"I can only tell you that I think so much of you. In these three years, I have come to love you, Lauren, for the wonderful woman that you are. We'll get your Philip back."

■ ■ ■

Josh and Philip entered the lab they had shared for the past three years. Josh quickly arranged the equipment. For the last time, they embraced.

"The other Philip will need you, Josh, if he returns. And I will miss you. When you accept that Nobel Prize for this work, know that your friend is with you, just out of reach."

Josh began the reaction. Just before it reached criticality, he recalled the unanswered question Lauren had posed to Philip as the two of them entered the kitchen. Lauren had asked Philip about his unusual goodnight message to their daughter, Marguerite. But Lauren had been distracted by Josh's presence, and Philip had not had a chance to answer.

"Philip," Josh said, "what was it you said to Marguerite when you put her to bed?"

"I told her that the world is not what she thinks it is, that it's way, way cooler than she could ever imagine, and to never forget that every moment is important. And then I kissed her goodbye."

■ ■ ■

Dr. Benjamin placed his hand on my right shoulder and leaned towards me. In a voice I have come to associate with truth and great wisdom, he added, "That's correct, Robert, the world is not what you think. Not even close. And that changes everything."

chapter one

CONTEMPLATION

Hopefully life is not as grim for us as it is for our universe-hopping character Philip. While we may be in the proper universe, we are not necessarily spared the burden of feeling that something about our lives is not quite right. How many of us are free from recurrent uncertainty and perhaps some anxiety about who we are and what we are supposed to do with this life we are granted? "What in the world has happened? How did I arrive at this place in the world?" you ask yourself. "Why is life so hard? What am I doing here? What's the point?" you wonder.

Only the most centered among us live without posing one of these questions, and exceedingly few without some anxiety about the person inhabiting their skin and how that person is to navigate a life. My own wife is one of those centered people. She harbors no anxiety about her place in this world. A confident woman, she is as comfortable with her weaknesses and blemishes as she is with her obvious gifts and strengths. If you were to ask her how she had arrived at this oasis of peacefulness, she would simply reply, "It's my faith."

My wife happens to be a Christian, but there are others like her, people of other faiths who share her inner peace and contentment and for whom anxiety is a foreign emotion. Collectively they have found strength in their concept of God and are quite willing to entrust their lives to God's will. What of the rest of us, the skeptical, for whom absolute faith is just not an option? Can we reach such heights without accepting "God's will" and without embracing one specific religious text? Are we destined to live anxious lives as we traverse life's hills and valleys, trying to figure out what we are supposed to be doing with the time we're allotted? Meaning and purpose are a reservoir of peace for my wife and other people of absolute faith—but where and how can the rest of us find it in our lives?

The great body of thought and literature surrounding these questions is called philosophy; those who pass their days embroiled in these issues are philosophers. Philosophers have arisen in every age, and they have developed theories and explanations for every facet of human existence. Some are religious figures, others secular. Many of these names are familiar, some less so—Plato and Aristotle, Descartes, Aquinas, Kierkegaard, Sartre—the list goes on and on. The truth, though, is that one need not be a Ph.D.-wielding college professor to contemplate these issues. Each and every one of us who has ever considered the question of the meaning or purpose of life is equally a philosopher.

Humanity's collective efforts to date have yielded no single great truth. There has been no moment of universal clarity, and the bells have not rung in every town and hamlet to signal the arrival of the one answer. That being the case, one might just recommend we forget the whole thing. Yet these questions—What is the point of life? Why are we here? —are the most important questions we can ask. Their answers are enormously powerful things, capable of changing the trajectories of cultures, nations and even civilizations. No questions are of greater significance to us, the six billion humans that inhabit the earth. How we act, what we do, how we treat each other and our planet—all of these issues are intricately entwined with the answers to these questions. If we only knew for certain if there was purpose to our lives and, if so, what specifically that purpose was, what a world of difference it would make.

Most would probably say that there is no way we can ever know. Only God knows, they insist. Perhaps they are correct. But because so many are unable to simply accept the unseen and unknowable and to yield to a higher authority, and because of the resultant turmoil in which our world is constantly embroiled, we have no choice. We must seek the answers. The other option—to throw our hands in the air and keep going blindly ahead in a world full of difficulty, sorrow, tragedy and limitless anxiety—is no option at all.

Why re-attempt what has repeatedly failed throughout history? Here is why: to make something far better of our existence, to suspend our inexhaustible efforts to destroy life—our own and that of others—and to create a world of love and peace, a world that can safely be enjoyed by generations to come.

Look around the world as this book is penned in 2009. There are the obvious ongoing conflicts in the Middle East, Afghanistan, Southeast Asia, Africa, South America, and even old Europe. On a less obvious but perhaps even more significant scale, bigotry and racism have not been eliminated, and like the influenza virus which for almost one hundred years has been relatively quiescent, they are poised to explode with new virulence at any moment. We cheat, we steal, we lie, we inappropriately judge, and we are violent without limit.

Technologically we are ascendant. We can communicate over unlimited distances at the speed of light. One can purchase just about anything from anywhere on the planet with a few clicks of a mouse. The world has become effectively much smaller. Incredibly, with all of this wondrous technology, we are in many ways no different than we were a thousand years past. The powerful still oppress the powerless in many parts of the world. Women are still denied education in far too many places. The poor have almost no chance of escaping the same fate as their equally poor ancestors. Tribalism is alive and thriving in many parts of the world. With the Internet and cell phones, with all of the computing power we have harnessed and the ability to share knowledge and information across the globe, how can such inhumanity and barbarism persist?

We have tried to tame humanity in so many ways, through calls for good will and warnings of eternal damnation. We have pleaded and begged both God and each other. We have invented religions of all sizes and shapes to meet the challenge. We have written and explained and analyzed ad nauseam, yet we still murder and abuse, rape and pillage, and destroy each other emotionally and physically.

Unlocking the mystery of life's purpose would define our existence individually and collectively. Imagine a world where we are all pulling in the same direction, where everyone knows and agrees on the route and the goal. Most would call an attempt to reach such a consensus a fool's errand, and I could not blame them. After thousands of years of civilization, in many ways we are no different than we were on Day One.

Why have we not succeeded in creating a world of peace and love, a world without violence, a world of compassion and kindness? There are multiple possible explanations; here are three to consider.

(1) This is simply who we are. Man is doomed by his nature. We were born to struggle and fail.

(2) Although we are perfectly capable of performing in a far better manner, it is God who insists that each of us struggle so that we may learn the requisite lessons. If God were to allow us to reach true peace and harmony, we would not have the opportunity to complete an education that can only be attained through personal challenges and hardships.

(3) Despite thousands of years of effort, we perpetually misinterpret our world. If we were to dramatically change our frame of reference, we could obtain the insight necessary to radically alter our individual and collective approach to life and create a world of peace and harmony.

Let's examine each of these options. First, are we in fact doomed by our nature? Many years ago I wrote a song entitled, "The Self-dooming Nature of Man" in which two protagonists argue the essence of man. One believes man is intrinsically good and has unlimited potential for love and creativity. The other claims that man is destined to fail, that he will inevitably succumb to his selfish desires, will kill, torture and do whatever it takes to survive and prevail. Here is the song's final verse:

"The trick my friend must be learned by you now,
it's his soul you must understand.
For there's nothing at all of justice,
just the self-dooming nature of man."

As a twenty-year-old I believed that we couldn't get out of our own way, that in fact mankind was preprogrammed for disaster. While there is plenty of historical evidence to suggest that this may be the primary program in play on this earth, there is also quite a bit of evidence to the contrary. Although the news is usually hijacked by reports of the ugliness of man against man, not a day passes without new stories of heroism and kindness. Countless people worldwide are actively helping their fellow man in the pursuit of justice and freedom, in developing and delivering medical care to those most in need, in bringing literacy and higher education to every nation on Earth, and by feeding the hungry and caring for the weak and frail. Literally millions upon millions of examples of stories grounded in kindness, compassion, incredible love and creativity speak against the theory that we are doomed to fail.

Our second option—the notion that we must struggle in order to learn the lessons for which God gave us life—is probably the most popular choice, especially among the world's organized religions. If we were all still in the Garden of Eden, this theory holds, we would never learn the distinction between good and evil. We would never experience the personal fulfillment that sacrificing for others can provide; we would never witness the personal growth that results when we overcome adversity. According to this worldly analysis, God is collectively holding us back from success for our own good. Too much peace and harmony, all love and no hate—in effect everyone holding hands and singing songs of friendship—would prevent us from individually learning the lessons of life that are required during our time on Earth.

Proponents of this theory explain the need for the dichotomies of life. We cannot appreciate warmth without cold, satiety without hunger, love without loneliness, empathy without pain. The clear message is that life is an education, and courses in pain and suffering are mandatory. While this theory would explain our inability to overcome our own jealousies and selfishness to create a world of peace and harmony, in my view it doesn't quite befit a rational deity, at least in its most popular form. I can't help but be skeptical of a God who would grant us so many wonderful gifts, chief among them the gift of love, and then require incredible levels of suffering to impress upon us the value of those gifts. While there is no doubt that there is much to learn during a life, blaming God for the suffering we inflict on each other seems unfair and incorrect.

Which brings us to the third option, the idea that we have made a collective and continuous error throughout our history; we have mis-interpreted our world. I am going to try to convince you that this is the best explanation for our failure (so far) to bring universal peace to our world. I hope to prove that there is every reason to believe that we have indeed perpetually misunderstood our reality.

We nod in agreement that ours should be a compassionate world, but secretly most people are convinced that in fact life is a zero-sum game, that my loss is your gain. Only the smart and strong soar; the weak just have to make do with whatever is left over. Over the centuries many have tried and failed to convince enough of the populace that this assumed truth is erroneous, that in fact love, compassion, caring and empathy trump fortune and power. Why have they failed to change peoples' minds and thereby affect behavior? Because it was always merely opin-ion, mine versus yours. If I claimed a "right" way to behave—if I preached that accumulating wealth and power at the expense of others was wrong—you could respond, "That's just your opinion."

As we will see in section I, "The World Is Not What You Think," no longer will that defense prevail. We will demonstrate that far more than human opinion is in play, and science will offer much of that proof. In section II, "What The World Is," we will employ the knowledge we gained in section I to reach deductions that once seemed unreachable.

I am by nature and training a skeptic and a scientist. What I have learned about our world, and what I will share with you in the pages to follow, derives from observation and logical deduction. It is neither wishful thinking nor naiveté; it is the way things really are. You will of course draw your own conclusions as we move through the book, as you should. I am buoyed by the knowledge that what I am about to present is an accurate representation of our world and our lives. Understanding this world paradigm will yield the opportunity to change what we can make of our collective existence. It will allow us to reach the harmony that has eluded us.

It would seem that a small work such as this would have no chance of reaching such unimaginable heights. True, it's a long shot, but then again history is filled with successful long shots. Man tried to fly for centuries before Wilbur and Orville figured it out, and their achievement, like so many others throughout history, is but one of innumerable examples of solving riddles that for so long seemed unsolvable. So with that spirit in mind, please turn the page: we begin now.

chapter two

FRAMING THE ISSUE

During my college years I became fascinated, as many college students do, with those theories of psychology and philosophy to which I alluded in chapter one. These disciplines are intimately entwined, and what makes them so seductive for the college-aged student is their very personal appeal. Just about all teenagers and young adults are narcissistic, but this should not be taken as criticism or judgment. It is as it should be, for those years are about self-discovery, a growing self-awareness, and a sense of wonderment about the world and our personal place within it. Psychology and philosophy, unlike economics or biochemistry, speak directly to the individual and seem to say, "I know what you are thinking about, and a great many who have come before you have wondered about the same things. Here are the answers you are looking for."

Without question, this is the voice I heard when I took these courses. I evaluated each theory, moving from Plato and Aristotle through the thinkers of the Reformation, from the rationalists to Freud and on to the behaviorists. I found all of them interesting, but none seemed to speak to my own personal inquiries and inclinations. Finally I found the existentialists, and I immediately knew that before me was an explanation of life that rang true. Why did this philosophical view, unlike so many of the others that had preceded it, immediately capture my attention? Here is an explanation from one of the most famous existentialists, Jean Paul Sartre:

> Man is nothing else but that which he makes of himself. That
> is the first principle of existentialism...Thus, the first effect of

19

existentialism is that it puts every man in possession of himself as he is, and places the entire responsibility for his existence squarely upon his own shoulders. And, when we say that man is responsible for himself, we do not mean that he is responsible only for his own individuality, but that he is responsible for all men. What we choose is always the better, and nothing can be better for us unless it is better for all. I am thus responsible for myself and for all men, and I am creating a certain image of man as I would have him to be. In fashioning myself I fashion man.

For me, a college student in the late 1960s and early 1970s, these concepts—that each man was responsible for defining his life, that we were not predestined or predetermined to be good or evil, and that each of us through our thoughts and deeds could influence the whole of humanity—were irresistible. Some existentialists believed in God, others like Sartre did not. But all of them believed that "existence preceded essence," that man was born a blank sheet of paper and was completely responsible to make his life, and the lives of his fellow man, meaningful. For months I walked the campus, lost in contemplation, thinking about Sartre and the other existentialists. I read Thomas Mann and Herman Hesse, German authors who explored the depth of the human experience. Life was heavy, but so meaningful.

All of this philosophy and deep thinking was wonderfully enlightening. I had arrived at college quite young and even more naïve, ridiculously inexperienced and severely uninformed on just about everything. I was literally starved for meaning and significance, and what better items on the menu for the intellectually starved than philosophy and psychology. But I was still just a teenager, and once my cerebral belly was full, my mind was at least temporarily freed, and I remembered what was really important: girls.

Just as it did for me, this interest in the meaning of existence wanes for most of us as we go on to seek careers and love interests. We become far more concerned with earning a living and the cute girl or guy we met at a party last weekend. Our attention slowly but inevitably turns to the mundane: getting a date and paying the bills, career enhancement, perhaps marrying and raising a family. Everyone's life evolves; the progression is well known. Life just happens, and off we go for the ride. What had seemed so important just a few years earlier now seems no more than the folly of a less-demanding time. Who has time for Sartre when you have to be up at six to get to work and fulfill your obligations in the office, only to hurry home to pick up the kids from soccer practice or attend a church meeting?

It's funny how we come to believe that these questions of life and its meaning, which may have preoccupied us previously, should ultimately be subjugated to the "really important" aspects of life, like family, career, and health. When a national tragedy occurs during football season, the announcer of the Sunday game never fails to inform us that such occurrences serve to remind us that football is only a game and will never compare in importance with issues of life and death. We take such statements as obvious facts, but are they really true? Is the announcer correct? Are sports less important than life and death issues? What *is* really important in life? Is it our family, our careers, and the health of our loved ones? It seems a ridiculous question, but who or what determines what is most valuable in life? If all life is random, and if we know that our lives are finite and our existences transient, then why should we assume that life and death issues are really any more important than whether or not our home team wins on Sunday? After all, we will all die someday. Is it really so critical whether that day arrives in five, fifty, or eighty years?

During the time that I was putting the framework for this book together, the famous columnist and humorist Art Buchwald wrote a short newspaper column from his hospice. Mr. Buchwald, terminally ill, addressed the issue of death and dying. His particular theme was what happens to us after we die. "Is there an afterlife or not?" he was asked by his friends. Mr. Buchwald wasn't sure, but if it made some people feel better to think that there was an afterlife, then that was fine with him, as was the converse. But what struck me about Mr. Buchwald's piece were the final two sentences. Here they are:

> The thing that is very important, and why I'm writing this, is that whether they like it or not, everyone is going to go. The big

question we still have to ask is not where we're going, but what were we doing here in the first place?

Bingo. This is the heart of the matter and the focus of this book. What in the world *are* we doing here in the first place? Why do we go to school, learn a trade to earn a living, get married, have children, and become part of a community? Why do we struggle to succeed, bear the burdens of illness and loss, and fight for what all too often in retrospect appear to be seemingly foolish goals? We all die—all of this is clearly only temporary—so why do we even bother to do these things and so many more when we already know the ending? Death is not an option, it is a certainty. The only uncertainties are the time, place, and circumstances of our demise. What then, for heaven's sake—should there be a heaven—is the point?

We are born, we strive to survive when survival is in doubt, and we strive to thrive when circumstances so permit. It is just what humans do. When one is hungry, cold, or terrified, as is so often the case for humans on our planet, pondering this question is, we would imagine, a luxury ill afforded. We may assume that only those who possess sufficient affluence to enjoy life with full stomachs and comfortable shelter might consider the question of a point to life worth investigating. But such a sentiment is almost certainly elitist and incorrect. Regardless of circumstance or station in life, most people ponder this issue from time to time, and more often than we might imagine. That is the power of this issue—in spite of hunger or dire circumstances, each of us senses that there is something more at play in this world, something strange and mostly inexplicable that lies beneath the surface of even the most difficult existence.

We are overwhelmed with potential concerns each and every day. Will I keep my job? Will I earn enough to pay the bills? Is my wife's illness serious, and will my kid pass his math test? Or worse, will my child be injured? And there is even that football team to worry about every Sunday. Our attention is spread thin as it is; how can we sacrifice any more of it for what appears to be solely a question of philosophy or metaphysics? For many, this is as far as the inquiry goes—a passing thought or an occasional gaze toward the heavens. We are aware of this question of the purpose of life, but that awareness slumbers in the deep background. We are content to leave such questions to the academics, who have ample time to ponder such ivory-tower issues while they polish off another Starbucks. Is it really worth my time, precious as it is, to even consider this issue?

It is, and here is why. The answer to Mr. Buchwald's question—the answer to why we are here in the first place—has the most profound effect on our lives and in fact on the entire planet. His question may be the most important question one can ask, and its answer the most critical of all responses. If we assume that all life is random, that in fact there is no rhyme or reason to human existence—or for that matter the existence of any living or inanimate object—then all hell may break loose without any lasting consequence. If the answer to the question of why are we here in the first place is "for no good reason," then nothing much matters. Freedom holds no advantage over tyranny, justice immediately becomes an irrelevant concept, and in fact each life is instantly devalued. Why would our behavior matter if all life is temporary and essentially meaningless? Kill as you please, take what you want from whomever you choose; in the end it makes no difference. We are here, we live a moment or a century, and we are gone. Our existence is hollow, our hopes and dreams foolish.

I cannot make the case to treat each other with love and compassion and to be our brother's keeper if there is no raison d'etre for our lives. I cannot ask myself or others to work hard to create beauty, to invent, and to enrich our minds and souls. I cannot ask the children to go to school, to have good manners, to treat others with respect and to earn respect as a result of their own behavior. What honest reason could I give for them to do so? If all begins as dust and ends as dust, if there is no great plan and life is just a series of loosely connected random events, then only the most pious would sacrifice anything for others. It would be near impossible to plead with humanity to do the right thing merely because we believed it the right thing to do. Who says what is the right thing, who decides, who really knows?

Having said all of that, one must admit that the possibility remains that we are indeed here for "no good reason." It is one of the legitimate available options to explain our presence on Earth. What *are* the potential explanations for our presence on this planet? Below is a short list to consider:

(1) There is a God, a deity who created us and maintains the world. God has granted life for a particular purpose.

(2) There is no God, just science. First there was the Big Bang, then a gigantic chemistry class, then evolution, and voila! Life. Our world is an unfolding chemical reaction. Life follows the rules of thermodynamics and is pretty much random.

(3) None of the above. The truth is something that we have not even imagined.

Upon reading the above choices, many people will instantly invoke God as the answer to this riddle. For the believers, the story goes something like this: God created man and woman, the heavens and the earth, and all of the creatures that share the world with us. God is the reason we are to treat each other with compassion and kindness; he has commanded us to do so. God knows best, and all things happen for a reason—even if as mere mortals we cannot possibly know or understand those reasons.

Let's first decide what we mean by "God." For those who choose to believe in a single deity, God is most often portrayed as a parent figure. It is possible that God is not so simple a character, not so easily defined by a single noun. God may be a far more complex concept. God may be a system, or an intricate series of systems. God need not be the simplistic concept with which we are so familiar in order to be a real entity.

But whatever form he does take and no matter how God is best described, God is probably the easiest answer to Mr. Buchwald's question. We are here because God put us here. We serve God. Man is inherently flawed, and only through service to God can we be redeemed. Of the six billion or so individuals inhabiting this planet, a majority accept some form of deity. Still, a significant minority remains for whom this answer does not suffice. Even those who do accept a deity do not always agree on God's plan or purpose. God is but one potential answer to our question.

The above list of three possibilities, while certainly not comprehensive, does give us an appropriate framework from which to proceed. Whether there are three possible answers or three hundred is not important. The number of possible answers to this central question of our reason for being is greater than one, and that is what matters. How then do we proceed to identify the correct answer?

Detective stories have always been popular, whether in books or on television or in the movies. Most have a similar construction. A seminal event occurs. As the story of this event unfolds, a mystery is uncovered that requires a solution. The protagonist and his or her accomplices set out to discover the truth, and to do so they assemble clues. At some point the clues—which upon initial discovery often appear random and unrelated—suddenly cohere and point to a unifying scenario, and the riddle is solved.

Our goal and methodology is no different as we seek to answer Mr. Buchwald's question. Some of the clues we seek are like footprints in the snow, clear signs that tell us that a moose or a bear has been in the area. Others will prove to be invisible at first, but as we become more aware they will reveal themselves, sometimes even leaping out to grab us. Clues are everywhere, in every action we take and in all of the events that fill our days. We may stumble upon them while performing the mundane chores of daily life or uncover them by looking into some of the less accessible corners of our minds and hearts. We will collect our clues, analyze them, and hope that at the conclusion of this journey we experience the epiphany that is the climax of all great mystery stories. Whenever we are about to uncover a clue, you will see this italicized sentence: SOMETHING IS GOING ON HERE.

What should we do with our time on Earth, what goals should we strive to achieve both individually and collectively? What matters in life? Which of our actions count for more, which for less? Is there a point to life, and at the end of the day does it really make any difference if there is or isn't?

These questions are not just interesting things to amuse ourselves with while enjoying a few beers with friends. Their answers will unveil a path that most of us are unfamiliar with, a path that is obscured by our habitually myopic vision. That which we have accepted as "truth" may prove to be erroneous. Our usual strategies may prove to be woefully inadequate, and our new understanding of our world something we have never imagined before. When we are done, "today" will mean much more than twenty-four hours, "now" will mean simply everything, and "life" will be a familiar term requiring a dramatically new definition.

chapter three

THE APPROACH

How are we to approach Mr. Buchwald's question, "Why are we here in the first place?" What strategy should we use to address this conundrum? Do we ask a million people, see what they think, and then take the most common answer and assume it to be correct? Do we convene a panel of experts in the fields of philosophy, biology, anthropology, cosmology, and psychology, have each of them take a shot, and then reach some sort of consensus? Do we analyze the great books of literature and religion and parse the verbiage until the answer leaps off of the page?

Asking a million people is not as crazy as it sounds. In his book *The Wisdom of Crowds*, James Surowiecki explains how large groups will often make far better decisions than a small group of experts if given only a minimum of information and the ability to decide independently. Mr. Surowiecki presents a compelling argument for group wisdom in the appropriate setting. People collectively somehow know a great deal, and they are more often correct than incorrect in their assessments—assuming they are not brainwashed or purposely led astray. How is this possible? This by itself is a clue to the mystery of why we are here, which we will explore later, but for now it is extremely helpful in defining our approach.

Rounding up a million people isn't so easy, and in fact getting large numbers to even respond honestly to a survey is no small task. As we have repeatedly witnessed, political polling is fraught with error. That's because the sample is never pure and totally unbiased; individuals don't always reveal their honest choice and sometimes just change their minds. I assembled a short questionnaire and distributed it to a broad sample of individuals. Three hundred twenty people completed this questionnaire. Below is the makeup of the respondents:

GENDER	RACE	AGE
Women–66%	Caucasian–80%	<25 5%
Men–34%	African American–12%	26–40 5%
	Asian–4%	40–55 47%
	Latino–1%	>55 17%
	Other–3%	

The survey contained sixteen questions. The first question presented three options, and respondents were asked to choose which of the three most closely represented their individual view of the world.

OPTION 1 (55%)	I am certain that there is a God as we know him through the concept of the major world religions. He knows our every thought and action and sets the ground rules for the world. God has created each of us for a purpose.
OPTION 2 (34%)	I would like to believe that there is a God who watches over us, but I need more evidence. It may be that there is a purpose to life, but maybe not. I'm just not certain.
OPTION 3 (11%)	I don't believe in God, at least not one who controls the world and our actions. There is no overall plan, no purpose, no deep meaning to any of our lives. We just are, like the Rocky Mountains and the sky above. We have no more purpose than a tree or a rock.

Our "crowd" answered as follows: 55% chose Option 1, 34% Option 2, and 11% Option 3.

The remaining fifteen questions posed statements, and respondents were asked to choose whether they agreed or disagreed with the statement or just were not sure.

I believe that life is a series of random events, there is no blueprint we follow, no overall point to it all.	22% agreed 55% disagreed 23% not sure
I believe that life is not random, and in fact most things happen for a reason. There are far fewer "coincidences" than we imagine.	67% agreed 19% disagreed 14% not sure
I believe that we are rewarded for our good behaviors, and punished for our bad behaviors.	48% agreed 31% disagreed 20% not sure
There is no single "right" way to behave. It's all a matter of personal opinion, and your opinion is no more valid than mine.	35% agreed 56% disagreed 10% not sure
There is a "right" way to behave, and that way is determined by God, not man.	37% agreed 51% disagreed 11% not sure
I believe that life evens out, "what goes around comes around." If you treat others poorly or are immoral, you will eventually pay the price.	75% agreed 12% disagreed 13% not sure
I believe that one of the major goals of life is to perform as many kind acts as possible, and that we each need to look out and care for each other.	89% agreed 3% disagreed 7% not sure
Sometimes I feel an inner power, or hear an inner voice, or have a sixth sense about the world that convinces me there is meaning and purpose to our lives.	59% agreed 23% disagreed 18% not sure
At least once I have felt a connection to a stranger or unknown place that I could not explain.	71% agreed 20% disagreed 9% not sure

I believe that our lives are not over after death. We live on in some way.	66% agreed 14% disagreed 20% not sure
I believe in ghosts, or that the dead are in some way still with us.	48% agreed 26% disagreed 25% not sure
There is a definite purpose to life. Each of us needs to make the most of our lives from what we are given.	86% agreed 5% disagreed 8% not sure
There is no overall purpose to life. What makes the most sense is to watch out for yourself and your family above all else.	13% agreed 69% disagreed 18% not sure
It doesn't make any difference if there is a purpose to life or not. It doesn't change anything. It's not worth thinking about.	8% agreed 83% disagreed 9% not sure
It is important to think about whether or not life has a purpose. How we choose to behave, how we spend our time, what we strive for, all depend on this question.	77% agreed 10% disagreed 12% not sure

This is not a scientific survey. The pool of respondents is small and skewed towards women and Caucasians. There is no income data or other indicators of socioeconomic status. Frankly, we know little about these respondents. However, that doesn't mean that there isn't a great deal to learn from their responses; although the survey is unscientific, the data are not irrelevant. In fact, it is more likely than not that the responses are representative of a far greater population, and allowing for a fairly wide standard deviation they probably reflect the attitudes and beliefs of a great many people. Since we are not looking for absolutes but rather clues, this data is very telling.

You have probably noticed that there is a good deal of redundancy in these questions—essentially the same question is asked in slightly different ways. When answering survey questions, many of us skim the words and may not take the time to fully understand what is being asked. Repeating the same question in various forms forces the respondent to rethink his or her response and—hopefully—provide the researcher with a more accurate reply.

What does our survey tell us? To begin with, our respondents are not sure about God. While the majority believe in a deity that in some way watches over the world, a large percentage of the respondents are just not certain. While the group as a whole may lean towards God as an explanation for our existence, it is not an overwhelming majority. That's important. The best we can say is that just over half are sure. Our "crowd" cannot definitely answer this one.

Why is that? Why didn't our respondents answer this most important question more definitively? And what is the significance of their inability to be more certain? It tells us that God is not the whole story for many. Most of us have been reared on God, if not in our particular family than at the least in our cultures. If so many remain uncertain, it is an indication that there may be something missing in our interpretation of God, something that would be necessary in order to explain our world and our existence to our satisfaction. A sizeable segment of our respondents just doesn't think that God as commonly interpreted is enough to explain the whole show. Of course, it may be that in fact God is the whole show but that we just haven't yet learned to make all of the connections.

What about the question of the randomness of life? Two questions, numbers five and six, address this issue, and the results tell us that two-thirds of the respondents believe that life is not random, that many coincidences are in fact something more. So although God is not a sure thing, the survey does produce a supermajority here: most of the respondents believe that something or someone is pulling the strings of life, and that the scientific laws of nature alone do not adequately explain events.

Questions seven through nine concern punishment and reward. Are we rewarded for good behaviors and punished for bad ones? Judging by the survey, many would like to believe that reward and punishment are logical, but when they are asked directly the response is mixed. The facts of life just don't seem to add up to such a simple plan in the eyes of many. But when we then move to question ten—which addresses the idea that life has a way of "evening out," or that what goes around comes around—the respondents are surprisingly uniform in their opinion. Three-quarters of respondents believe this to be the case, that if you act poorly you will eventually "get yours." This may seem to be at odds with the answers to the prior questions concerning reward and punishment. If one believes that we eventually pay a price for our behaviors, then how can that same person reject the idea that there is punishment and reward for our behaviors? Could it be that, generally speaking, people are more certain of punishment than they are of reward? In other words, act poorly and pay the price; act appropriately, and you may or may not see any direct benefit.

Question eleven is the feel-good question of the group. Almost 90 percent agree that performing acts of kindness is a major goal of life. Wow! Hope is indeed eternal, for in a world where such a large majority believes in caring for others, the future must always shine brightly. People want to do good things for others. Our survey clearly demonstrates a strong urge to do so, and this is no surprise. If one asks for help, with both sincerity and kindness, then the response is usually overwhelmingly positive. We enjoy helping each other.

We may ask ourselves about the possible motivation for this enthusiasm. Is it because performing good works improves the probability of future personal benefit, either here or in some great beyond? We have already seen that our group is, as a whole, not sure about the probability of reward for good behaviors. One could argue that it is actually selfish, rather than selfless, to act in a kind and generous manner. Doing good deeds usually makes us proud, raises our self-esteem, and in the end creates happiness. Almost all would agree that this form of "selfishness" is just fine, because the result is overwhelmingly positive for all involved.

This sense of service could be genetic, something that is wired into us at a deep level. In fact other authors have insisted that this is so. On the other hand, it remains possible that this desire to help others is an acquired trait, something learned through continual exposure to a set of attitudes occurring within organized societies and religions. While this possibility cannot easily be refuted, it seems more likely that there is something inherently "right" about caring for others, something instinctive in the human genome. Kindness transcends cultures and societies; it's something that seems native to our species. Why is it so? Why have we evolved with this inborn sense that to do good for others is correct?

SOMETHING IS GOING ON HERE.

We have uncovered an apparent truth. Overwhelmingly, people believe that doing good deeds and helping others is desirable. As we mentioned, this urge seems to transcend religions and cultures. Even though we certainly don't act upon this urge often enough—war, violence against others, degradation, and cruelty all persist—we have some collective sense that it is right to care for others.

"Some collective sense." This phrase is important. While each of us may act at times in a manner that is antithetical to the principle of the golden rule—to treat others as you would wish to be treated—still, we collectively embrace this concept. I am certain that this attitude, this desire to look out for one another, preceded Jesus and has been part of human nature since mankind's earliest days. Some might say that this is evolutionary, that it arose to protect the species. Maybe, but one could just as easily argue that it runs counter to the concept of survival of the fittest. Why would the strong support the weak? We currently cannot definitively answer this question, but we do know that this collective sense of caring for each other is very real. It comes from somewhere, and we must seek its origin.

Questions twelve and thirteen address the unseen. A sixth sense, the sensation that an event has occurred before, hearing an inner voice, sensing a connection to a stranger or an unknown place—all of these have been described over the centuries and continue to be described today. Seventy percent of our respondents have felt some type of connection to an unfamiliar person or place. This is surprising. Almost three out of four have had such an experience in their lives, one that they could not explain. What is this all about? I have never been one for ghost stories, but over the years I have learned to keep an open mind. Once again, SOMETHING IS GOING ON HERE. It is not possible to merely shrug off the experiences of a group of this size. We can draw no specific conclusions from these vague experiences, but we do not need to at this moment. We only need to know that a great many people intermittently experience sensations of closeness, familiarity, or connection when in unfamiliar settings or when meeting new people. But that's enough to generate another clue.

What about life after death? Is there a hereafter, or does life just end with a whimper and that's all there is? Two-thirds of our respondents believe in some form of life after death, and only 14 percent doubt the possibility. The remaining people are undecided. Less than half, though, believe that the dead are still with us in some form or another. This implies that our cohort believes in a separation between the living and dead, and that the dead are not walking among us in some twilight zone.

It's nothing new to suggest that lots of people believe in a hereafter of some kind. We like to believe that the certainty of death does not mean the end of life; we like to believe that there are better days ahead. Such thinking is completely natural, but if we force ourselves to be objective, to abandon our deepest hopes and to clinically debate this question, we would admit that proof of a hereafter is quite scarce, if not completely absent. Of course there are those who practice séances, people who believe that they can communicate with the departed. For the rest of us, there is essentially no hard evidence of a hereafter. True, we have no proof of the converse, but that is a weak argument. The burden of proof, if that's what you're looking for, is clearly on those who believe in a hereafter.

Nevertheless, most people—just like two-thirds of our respondents—have a sense that there may be some kind of "continuation" after death. This fact reminds us of that inexplicable and collective sense of caring for others which we discussed a few paragraphs above. Here's a good rule. While two-thirds of any group can easily be wrong, watch out when they come to the same conclusion independently. In situations where a group is not clearly influenced by a few—a group whose individual members are shielded from each other—the group as a whole is surprisingly wise. So although we should not accept that there is indeed a hereafter of some sort based on the opinions of two hundred people, we might wish to pay some attention and recognize a clue when we see one. SOMETHING IS GOING ON HERE.

Our final group of questions, questions sixteen through nineteen, deal with the question of a purpose to life, which is the theme of this book. Eighty-six percent tell us they believe that there is a definite purpose to life, and 83 percent deny that this question is irrelevant to how we live. Over three-quarters agree that we need to think about this question of life's purpose, because it affects our lives in multiple ways.

I find this section of the survey and these responses quite incredible. It is so easy in Western societies to become jaded as we watch television and movies, read the newspapers or magazines, or surf the web. So much of their content seems to suggest that we Westerner's collectively accept that the purpose of life is to party and to get famous and rich. We would be mistaken to accept this assumption, because if we were to hand out this survey to thousands of people in first-world cities and let them respond privately and anonymously, I would bet the results would not be dramatically different than what we found in our small sample.

Our habits of speech and action may seem to hint at a certain disdain for living a purposeful life; nevertheless, the apparently widely held belief in a purpose for life lies just a bit beneath the surface, and I believe that secretly, at a level we're only dimly aware of, we are anxious to free it from the shadows. As a society, we have moved away from some core human concepts. But we want to believe that there is more to life than the mundane and unending stream of challenges each of us confronts on a daily basis.

Why do we want this? Why is it in us?

SOMETHING IS GOING ON HERE. And it smells like another clue to me.

One more item needs to be mentioned as we conclude this examination of our small survey. The responses were surprisingly uniform across all age groups. For me this was a surprise, as I had assumed that younger people would be more likely to favor a random model of life. Life experience, I thought, must certainly be a prerequisite for embracing the concept of a non-random and more purposeful existence. Yet this is apparently not the case. Are we somehow hard-wired with some of these concepts? Once again, SOMETHING IS GOING ON HERE.

While this is a very small, unscientific sample, there is very important information in these three hundred twenty responses. We have our first set of clues. These are what I would term "soft" clues because they are difficult to empirically prove. We will encounter more of these in chapter six. By themselves, soft clues are easy to ignore, but when coupled with the hard clues we will discover in the next chapters, they take on much greater significance. The game is on!

chapter four

THE HARD CLUES— RELATIVITY

"The overarching lesson that has emerged from scientific inquiry over the last century is that human experience is often a misleading guide to the true nature of reality...the insights of modern physics have persuaded me that assessing life through the lens of everyday experience is like gazing at a van Gogh through an empty Coke bottle."
—BRIAN GREENE, *The Fabric of the Cosmos*

We now temporarily leave the realm of soft clues and begin to explore clues based in fact. This chapter is about space and time, and more specifically it is about something called the theory of relativity. Why am I interested in space and time? Why am I asking you to also become interested in this seemingly obscure topic? *The World Is Not What You Think* is the title of this section of the book. I am not a physicist, and the explanations that follow in this and the following chapter are not meant to replace books on these topics written by true experts. My goal in these two chapters is to demonstrate that some of the most fundamental concepts in our lives, principles that we just accept as fundamental to our reality, are in fact not at all as they appear to be. Time and space are two such principles.

First a warning is in order. What we will discuss in this chapter and the one that follows can be quite confusing. Please don't worry if you don't follow every nuance of the discussion. No exam is required, and if you find this material too esoteric or difficult, rest assured that you are far from alone. For our purposes, it matters only that you come away from these chapters with a sense that time, space, and the laws that govern the universe are more interesting and much different than you assumed, and that the physical world is not what it appears to be.

We take for granted that time marches on relentlessly, that it's the same for you and me no matter where we are, whether sleeping comfortably in our beds or driving down a highway. We also assume that space just *is*. By space I mean all of the universe—our Earth, the planets and stars, the intervening void between them, and even just the distance from one place to another. We don't need to think about space; we just occupy it. If we measure the length of an object or the distance between two objects, we feel confident that no matter how often or under what circumstances we repeat that measurement, it will be the same. Space and time, two very basic components of our existence, seem pretty solid and unchanging. As it turns out, they are neither. Space and time are in fact quite mysterious.

Let's begin with time. I am completely overwhelmed by time. It's not that I don't have enough time (I don't), or that I waste time (I do). It's the nature of time that overwhelms me. What *is* time?

For one thing, time is a dimension. It is descriptive. Let's say I wish to meet a friend for dinner at my favorite restaurant. He would need to know a few pieces of information to arrive at that appointment. First, he would need to know the location of the restaurant, which is just a specific latitude and longitude on the globe. A street address will do. Since the restaurant is on the fourth floor of a high-rise building, he would also need to know the height off of the ground (the elevator knows that precise information, so practically he would need only the floor number). The last piece of information is the time of our dinner. Time is the well-known fourth dimension.

So far we have no problem. Time is a dimension just as length, width, and height, and surely those are not overwhelming for anyone. Yet we all know that time is different than those other dimensions. Length, width, and height don't cause us anxiety. We don't change from one meter to the next as we do from one moment to the next. We can almost always choose to return to a specific place, but time does not afford us that luxury. Time seems to go in one direction—forward. While we can travel to or from a destination, or go up or down in an elevator, we can't go to sleep today and wake up yesterday.

Unless you are a physicist, you would likely agree that time passes the same for all of us, that the clock ticks the same for you and me. But that is not how time works. The truth is that time is not a constant; our clocks are not necessarily synchronized. If you are in a plane traveling at six hundred miles per hour, zooming across North America while I am reclining on my couch watching my favorite movie, the clock will tick more slowly for you than it will for me. If, just before you take off on your flight, we both simultaneously click our stopwatches and let them run for one hour, I will declare that one hour has passed ever so slightly before you make the same claim. In 1905, Albert Einstein proved this to be true. Time dilation, as this phenomenon is technically known, is one of the effects predicted by his theory of special relativity. Time actually passes at a different rate for each of us depending on whether we are at rest or whether we are moving, and the size of the discrepancy depends upon the speed at which we are moving. Just why this is so and how this works are confusing, and I will do my best to explain this just ahead.

First of all, how did Einstein come to this concept? About ten years before he published his famous paper on special relativity, a discovery was made, one which proved that the speed of light is always measured to be the same, no matter how fast one is moving. We can use an example to explain this idea.

If I am standing along the side of the road and you drive by in a car at sixty miles per hour, and if I use a radar gun to measure your speed, I will of course record your speed as being sixty miles per hour. But if instead of standing at rest along the roadside I am traveling alongside you in another car which is also moving at sixty miles per hour, it will seem to both of us that we are not moving, since relative to each other we aren't. If I take a measurement of your speed from my car, my radar gun would register zero miles per hour. We are moving along in the same direction and at the same speed; there is no "difference" for the gun to measure.

I am going to introduce an equation with which we are all familiar. The equation is: speed (or velocity) = distance divided by time. The formula would look like this:

speed (v) is distance (d) divided by time (t):
$$d/t = v$$

If you walk ten miles (d, your distance traveled), in two hours, (t, your time), then your speed (v) is five miles per hour:

10 miles (d) / 2 hours (t) = v 5 miles / hour (miles per hour)

Let's apply this to our car example. When I measure the speed of a passing car with my radar gun, the radar gun is in fact solving that equation (though using calculus instead of simp le math, but the principle is the same). It is measuring the distance the car traveled, d, divided by the time it took the car to travel that distance, t, and telling us the speed, v. When I measure the moving car while I am standing still, the radar gun calculates the distance that the car traveled in a period of time, solves the equation and gives me the result of sixty miles per hour. When I get into a second car and travel at sixty miles per hour in the same direction as the target car and then attempt to measure the speed of that car, the radar gun sees that the target car does not travel any distance at all relative to me—we are moving at the same speed, next to each other. And so it measures a speed of zero.

Now let's repeat the same experiment, but instead of measuring the speed of a car, let's measure the speed of a beam of light. The term "speed of light" means how far a light beam will travel, d, in a certain amount of time, t. If I am standing still and measure the speed of the light beam, I will record a speed of 186,282 miles per second—this is often rounded off, for the sake of convenience, to 186,000 miles per second. If once again, just as in the prior experiment, I then get in a car traveling in the same direction as the light beam—in fact a super car that can travel at a speed of 186,000 miles per second—and if I once again measure the speed of that light beam next to me, you would think that my radar gun would measure the speed of the beam to be zero miles per second, since just as we saw in the preceding car example there is no relative difference between our speeds. But that is not what my radar gun says. It says that light beam is traveling at 186,000 miles per second, the same number I got when I was standing still. You can repeat that experiment while you are traveling at any speed, and you will get the same measurement for that light beam—186,000 miles per second, the speed of light, every time.

How can we explain the remarkably different results of the car experiment and the light beam experiment, and what does it all mean?

The second experiment—the one where I was in my super car moving at the same speed as the light beam—represents the thought experiment that Einstein performed in his head. Recall that years before his epiphany, experiments had proven that the speed of light never changed, no matter how fast the observer of that light beam was moving. Einstein, of course, was aware of this discovery, and he therefore recognized that no matter how fast he was going—even if he were riding a second light beam and traveling himself at the speed of light—he would measure that other light beam's speed to be the speed of light, 186,000 miles per second. In order for that to be so, *something else* must have been changing.

Let's bring back the formula from above:

speed (v) is distance (d) divided by time (t): $d/t = v$

Since in the two experiments I measured v, the speed of the light beam, to be the same both when I was moving and when I was stationary, something else in that equation has to be changing. What must be changing is one of the other two parts of that equation—the distance traveled by the light beam, d, or the time it took for that light beam to travel that distance, t, or both. This in essence is Einstein's great revelation: the fact that one always measured the same speed for light, no matter whether the observer was at rest or moving at any speed, meant that distance and time had to be the things that were changing. It has to be that way for the equation to balance.

Let's perform another experiment to illustrate Einstein's ingenious discovery. You and I are standing beside one another, neither of us moving, and you are holding a stick. We each have a tape measure, we each measure that stick, and we both agree that it measures one meter. Now let's say I put you on a high-speed moving sidewalk like those found in an airport, except that this one moves very quickly—it can transport you at one-third the speed of light. As you zoom past me (I am standing still), I take a snapshot of your stick and make a measurement of its length. I measure your stick at about one-half meter long. This seems a bit bizarre to me, since while we were both at rest I measured that stick to be one meter in length. So I check my measurement again, and sure enough, I still get a half-meter. At the same time that I am measuring your stick, you are also measuring the same stick while you and the stick are cruising along happily together on the high-speed moving sidewalk. But you measure it to be one meter long, the same result we both got when we were at rest. So as I stand still and measure your stick to be a half-meter in length, you and the stick whiz by me, and your measurement shows it to be one meter in length. So which is it? Is the stick one meter or one-half meter? Who is correct, you or me?

We both are. The measurement differs because we are moving at different speeds relative to each other. Crazy, right? This is one of the conclusions that Einstein deduced in 1905 with his famous thought experiments. Length contraction—the changing result of measurement dependent on the relative speed of the observer and the object being measured—has since been proven many times over by experimentation. We will measure the length of objects differently if we are moving at different speeds. Absolute distance does not exist.

Just as length varies according to the speed of the observer relative to the object being measured, as our experiment with the meter stick demonstrates, so too is time relative. Our clocks do not all tick at the same rate. This has significant implications for our notion of time. What a stationary observer takes to be two simultaneous events may not be measured as such by another observer who is in motion. Since time is different for each of us depending upon the speed at which we are moving, what constitutes "now" for each of us is not the same.

A simple example will help with this difficult concept. Let's say you and I are standing next to each other in the middle of a football field at the fifty-yard line, halfway from each of the goalposts. On each goalpost a lamp has been hung. The lamps are on the same circuit, so when the switch is turned on, both lamps turn on simultaneously. You give the signal and the switch is thrown. We are each wearing helmets which house a sensor that records the light from each goalpost lamp, and when you call for the goalpost lamps to be turned on, our helmets each record the time that the two light beams reached us. We both measure the same result, that the light from each lamp arrived simultaneously.

For the next part of the experiment one of us will no longer stand still. I start to run toward the goalpost to our right, and you give the signal for the lamps to be turned on. This time, when we review the information from our helmets, we see that for me the light on the goalpost lamp *towards* which I am running—the one to our right—reached my helmet before the light from the goalpost lamp to our left. Since I was running towards the right goalpost, the light from that goalpost lamp had a shorter distance to travel than the light from the left goalpost lamp, so it arrived at my helmet before the light from the left goalpost lamp did. Since you remained motionless at the middle of the field, your helmet received both light beams at the same time. What appeared to be simultaneous to you—both lamps illuminating at the same moment—was not simultaneous for me. For me, the light from the right goalpost lamp illuminated first. What you would describe as what happened at a particular moment in time is different than what I would describe. It is the same event, but there are two different experiences. We are both completely correct in terms of our experience. Neither of us is more correct than the other.

This simple experiment illustrates a very important concept. What any one person describes as the current moment—his or her "now"—can be different for someone else who is moving at a different speed. There is no such thing as one "now." "Now" depends on one's particular frame of reference. As it turns out, this has far-reaching implications. In our football field experiment, I was running quite slowly, especially relative to the speed of light. Therefore the difference between the arrival times of the two light pulses was miniscule, and in fact was not noticeable to anything other than a sensitive instrument. If instead the difference in relative speed between observers is great, the discrepancy can be huge.

Brian Greene, the author of the quote at the beginning of this section and a professor of physics and mathematics at Columbia University in New York, says this in his book, *The Fabric of the Cosmos*:

> Observers moving relative to each other have different conceptions of what exists at a given moment, and hence they have different conceptions of reality.

Different conceptions of reality. That is a powerful statement. What this says is that our experiences are not uniform. What we interpret as "now" is not universal. Reality is truly in the eye of the beholder, and not just because we interpret reality differently based on emotions or prejudices. The laws of physics tell us that we actually do interpret reality differently if we are moving relative to each other.

Here is another way to look at this issue, another excellent perspective I am borrowing from Professor Greene. The sum of one's speed through *space* plus one's speed through *time* is equal to *the speed of light.* What in the world does that mean? If you are standing still, none of your motion is through space; all of your motion is through time. You are therefore moving through time at the speed of light. Next, instead of standing still, you climb into your new Mercedes sports car and zoom off at a hundred miles per hour. Now some of your motion is through space, and so your speed through time has diminished by that hundred miles per hour—not a very significant amount since light moves along at a pretty good clip, over 186,000 miles per second. Suppose instead that you are zooming through space on a brand new state-of-the-art starship at 18,600 miles per second. Your speed through time is then reduced by 10 percent (since 18,600 is 10 percent of 186,000). In other words, your motion through time has slowed down since you are now no longer stationary but are moving through space and *have converted some of your motion through time to motion through space.* Your clock really would tick more slowly than the clock of someone back on Earth who is not moving, since 100 percent of that stationary person's motion is through time. Since time is passing more slowly for you than it is for him, you would age more slowly than he would. It is really true that someone sent off in a spaceship at a velocity approaching the speed of light for a ten-year period—five years outbound, five years inbound—would age far less than the ten years aged by someone who had remained on Earth. Truth is indeed stranger than fiction!

A light beam presents an interesting issue. It is moving by definition at the speed of light (it is light!) and therefore all of its motion is through space and none is left to move through time. The result: a light beam never ages! If you were to hop a ride on a laser beam, you would remain forever young. In fact, light particles experience just this phenomenon. A particle of light leaves a distant star 100,000 light years away. That means it would take 100,000 years for that particle, moving at the speed of light, to reach Earth. But that's if we here on Earth are the ones doing the measuring. For that light particle, which travels at the speed of light, time stands still. Remember, for anything moving at the speed of light, all of its motion is through space and none through time; no time passes for that object. So that particle of light, from its point of view, seems to move from its star of origin to Earth—an incredible distance away—instantaneously!

The point of this brief and confusing exercise is that time is anything but simple to understand, and in fact is quite mysterious. Let's think about time, let's say for a moment. What is a moment? When is a moment "the present?" When does that moment slide into the immediate past? What does it mean for it to be in the immediate future? We imagine time as a timeline, the kind most of us learned in school.

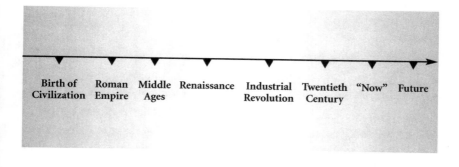

| Birth of Civilization | Roman Empire | Middle Ages | Renaissance | Industrial Revolution | Twentieth Century | "Now" | Future |

Way to the left of this timeline is the birth of civilization in Mesopotamia, followed by the Romans, the Middle Ages, the Renaissance, and the Industrial Revolution. Moving to the right, we encounter the more recent past, the twentieth century, and the present. We assume that the past is just that—past and gone. If we imagine our timeline as a movie, only the frame showing the current moment would be illuminated; everything in the past would be dark, as if the only moment that is actually real and alive is the present moment. Everything to the left of today is what we call history. It's in our past somewhere and is relevant to us only in terms of our personal memories or as a historical lesson. Of course there is also the future, everything to the right of "now" on our timeline. In our usual way of thinking about time, the future is blank and formless, composed of events that are yet to occur.

It turns out that this concept of time—a past which lies in the dark, already happened and gone; an illuminated now; and a blank future—is without doubt completely incorrect. Suppose I tell you that the past is just as alive as the current moment. On top of that, suppose I also claim that the future, that which has yet to occur and which lies on the far right of our timeline, is also just as alive as the current moment. Equating an unseen future with a well-documented past seems at the minimum unusual if not bizarre and impossible. But that is precisely what Einstein's theory of special relativity proclaims. Once you accept that clocks tick differently depending on our speed through space, and once you accept that what we take to be simultaneous events are in fact not necessarily so, you have accepted the fact that all moments, in a sense, coexist.

Crazy stuff, but true. SOMETHING IS GOING ON HERE. What is that something? First of all, time is not the past, the present, and the future as we are used to assuming. In fact, it is all present—the past is not dead and gone. A better way to think about time is that every moment exists forever—not just in our memories, but also for real. While we can't just jump in a time machine and race back to that fabulous vacation in Hawaii we had last summer, those days are still very much alive. They are in our past in the sense that we are no longer experiencing that vacation, but that moment in time never really goes away.

Imagine time as a loaf of bread. Each moment of time is a slice of that bread. As we move from moment to moment, we experience another slice, but the preceding slices don't disappear. They are still just as real as they were before they were experienced, just as real as they were at the moment of the experience, and they will stay real no matter how far we travel forward in time. Time is the loaf of bread that cannot be consumed.

The moments of time are infinite. We imbue some moments with far greater importance than others—religious and secular holidays, birthdays—but when taken as a group, moments can not be differentiated from each other. In our loaf of bread, there is no one slice that is more special than another; they all coexist equally and simultaneously. Our "special" moments are only special because we decide from our own perspective, from our own vantage point, that they are. We create illusions about these moments. I mention this point only briefly here, but it is in fact quite critical to our exploration, and we will return to this issue a bit later.

To summarize this bizarre concept of time, here again is Professor Brian Greene. This paragraph is worth reading more than once.

> So: if you buy the notion that reality consists of all the things in your freeze-frame mental image right now, and if you agree that your now is no more valid than the now of someone located far away in space who can move freely, then reality encompasses all of the events in space-time. The total loaf exists. Just as we envision all of space as really being out there, as really existing, we should also envision all of time as really being out there, as really existing too. Past, present, and future certainly appear to be distinct entities. But as Einstein once said, 'For we convinced physicists, the distinction between past, present, and future is only an illusion, however persistent.' The only thing that's real is the whole of space-time … In this way of thinking, events, regardless of when they happen from any particular perspective, just are. They all exist. They eternally occupy their particular point in space-time. There is no flow (of time)…every moment (in time) is illuminated, and every moment remains illuminated. Every moment is.

Under close scrutiny, the flowing river of time more closely resembles a giant block of ice with every moment forever frozen in place.

The first few times I read Brian Greene's words, I said *wow!* It was the only sound I could utter. Many years ago, well before I had any interest in or knowledge about relativity, I told my wife that I had a sense that all time was co-existent. One day I decided to learn something about Einstein's relativity, and it was then that I was exposed to this incredible truth about our universe. This is not New Age thinking or metaphysical wishing and hoping; this is hard science, real physics. There is no such thing as absolute time, and there is no absolute distance. Past, present, and future are all coexistent. Time does not flow, it just is. And it is different for each of us. My now and your now are not the same if one of us is moving at all. Time and space are not what we thought, period. The world is not what you think!

Before we leave this discussion of space and time, I want to offer you one more fact about our world. You may have noticed that there is something unusual about light, specifically the speed of light. We have seen that we always measure its speed to be the same, no matter our own speed—which is quite a different result than what we find when we measure the speed of things like cars. Light is indeed quite special. The speed of light, 186,000 miles per second, is as fast as anything can go. You can always get a car or a plane or a spaceship to go just a bit faster if you try hard enough, but once you get to the speed of light, that's it. In fact, if you try to get something moving at the speed of light, it becomes infinitely massive, so massive that it can no longer be moved. The speed of light is a limit; nothing can exceed that speed limit. Why? It is an excellent question, one without a clear answer. If one were to somehow exceed the speed of light, funny things would happen with time, and that is not permitted in the world we know.

Everything you have just read in this chapter is true. It's likely that you find it a bit crazy, and even unsettling. Nevertheless, it is all completely true. Time and space are not what we have imagined them to be.

We are going to leave time and relativity for now, though I promise you we have not heard the last of them. Before we discuss the significance of these amazing truths, we are going to look at some other "hard clues" that are equally if not even more amazing. So if your mouth is still agape, take a moment to rest your facial muscles, because in the next chapter you will need them again.

chapter five

THE HARD CLUES—
THE QUANTUM WORLD

Y ou may have heard the terms "quantum physics" and "quantum mechanics" before, but many people have not. And few people have any idea, really, what these ideas are all about. Quantum physics describes the realm of the very small, and here I mean really, really small. It is concerned with things far smaller than atoms, things smaller than even the protons that make up the nucleus of the atom. So right away you may be wondering how something so small—how things we cannot even see—can have anywhere near the impact you might be anticipating considering the buildup I just gave it at the end of the prior chapter on relativity.

First, we have to talk about certainty versus uncertainty. The sun rises in the east and sets in the west, we will all die, and then there are those annoying taxes. We actually take quite a bit more as certain. We assume that we can make precise predictions about lots of things in our lives. Our world is in many ways predictable: if we do x, then y will happen. If we drop a raw egg on a tile floor, it will crack. If we throw a ball in the air, it will fall back into our hands.

Well, here we go again. It turns out that quantum physics (a synonym for quantum mechanics) proves that we actually can't predict anything with certainty; the best we can do is give any outcome a probability. Everyone's personal experience is that we perform millions of actions every day, and we pretty much know how they will turn out, just like our cracking egg and falling ball. The field of quantum physics, which is less than a hundred years old, has proven without question through numerous exacting experiments that in fact nothing is completely certain in this world, absolutely nothing. This concept of probability versus certainty is one of the fundamental ideas behind quantum physics, and we will spend some time explaining this phenomenon and looking at examples.

Our first encounter with the quantum world involves light and the question of whether light is a wave, like an ocean wave, or whether it is made up of discrete particles, like baseballs. "Who cares?" would be a reasonable response to that question, but it turns out that this issue is incredibly important for understanding how our world actually works.

I am going to borrow some examples from the physicist we met in the last chapter, Brian Greene, author of *The Fabric of the Cosmos*, who in my view is the writer who most clearly articulates the concepts of quantum physics for the non-physicist. We are all familiar with the waves created in a lake when a rock is dropped into the water. Multiple concentric circles are generated, emanating from the center where the rock hit the water. The circles are waves which are composed of alternating high points, the peaks, and low points, the troughs. Now let's imagine that you are standing on one edge of the lake and I am standing across from you on the other side, and that we both start dropping rocks into the water. Eventually our concentric circles will meet; the waves we have created will start to bump into one another.

Where two peaks collide—one peak from the waves I created and the other from the waves you created—the result is a new peak that is twice as tall and which is a combination of our two peaks. Where two troughs meet, the result is a trough that is twice as deep. And when a peak meets a trough, they cancel out and the water is flat. This illustrates what is known as an interference pattern. Interference patterns are seen wherever waves of any sort interact with each other. This includes water waves, sound waves, light waves, and other kinds of waves in other mediums; when we see alternating peaks, troughs, and areas where peaks and troughs cancel out, we know we are dealing with waves. While the peaks and troughs are easy to see with water waves, the effect is somewhat different with light waves. Interfering light waves will produce peaks and troughs just as the water waves do, but they will look like alternating bands of light and dark. Light bands are areas where either two peaks or two troughs meet, while dark bands are areas where peaks and troughs meet and cancel each other out.

In order to determine whether light is best described as wave-like or particle-like, an experiment known as the double-slit experiment can be performed. For this experiment, we need a piece of photographic film, and we will need to scratch two vertical slits into the film to allow light to pass through. The slits should be closely spaced. Add a source of light, such as a laser beam, and place a screen behind the piece of film to record the results of the light passing through the slits, and we are ready to begin. If we shine the laser onto the piece of film with the slits and then examine the light that gets through the slits and hits the screen behind the piece of film, we will see alternating light and dark bands, indicative of a wave pattern. The light bands represent combined peaks or combined troughs of the waves, the dark bands the places where peaks and troughs cancel each other out. Such a pattern provides proof that light acts as a wave, since we are seeing a typical interference wave pattern. What this implies is that the laser light spreads out and passes through both slits; that is the only way to explain the interference pattern produced on the screen. The waves of light passing through each slit bump into each other like our concentric circles in the lake and create the interference pattern. Seems pretty simple so far: light is a wave.

Let's now change the experiment a bit. First, instead of film we need a piece of metal with two slits separated by a small distance. Instead of a laser beam, we will fire electrons, one electron at a time. (Electrons are negatively charged particles that are found in all atoms. They are also responsible for the image on our television screens.) We also need a special screen placed behind the metal that will light up when it is hit by our electrons. Since each of these small electrons is a particle, like a BB or a baseball, and since we have two slits on the metal, each particle needs to choose which slit it wants to go through, left or right—or no slit at all, in which case it will just bounce off the metal.

We start firing off our individual electrons, and once we have fired off a good number of electrons we need to look at the screen behind the metal to see just what pattern shows up on the screen. Since these are discrete particles, we would expect to see one band behind each slit, which would represent the buildup of the particles that passed through that particular slit, just as we would expect if we were throwing baseballs or shooting BBs through the slits. But that's not what we find. In fact we see alternating dark and light bands, those same peaks and troughs we saw before when we used the laser beam. And just as before, the bands aren't concentrated in any one place—they alternate, all the way across the screen. They are telling us once again that we must be dealing with waves.

Wait a minute. Weren't we firing individual electrons through those slits? How can electrons—which are discrete particles—behave as waves? That's an excellent question. We just learned that anytime you see an interference pattern it means that you are dealing with waves. If we are getting an interference pattern while shooting individual electrons through these slits, then each electron must be acting as a wave—which means it must be going through *both* slits at the same time, not just one. What seems to be a discrete particle actually somehow behaves like a wave. Although this is a bit unsettling and difficult to explain, we can't argue with the facts of our experiment.

The story becomes even more incredible. We can perform the same experiment using individual photons, the smallest packet of light, instead of electrons. When we do so, we find precisely the same result, the alternating light and dark bands, confirming that we are dealing with waves.

Now let's add a new wrinkle to our experiment. (Although the experiment I will describe now actually employs a more complex apparatus, we will stick with our double slit setup, since for our purpose it is equivalent.) We will place a special detector—sort of a toll booth—in *front* of each slit. That way we can know which slit each photon passed through, or if it somehow passed through both— in which case it would trigger both detectors. We perform the exact same experiment, using a photon source firing individual photons, our piece of metal with two slits, and the screen behind. And now we place a highly accurate and sensitive detector in front of each slit. We turn on these detectors and begin to fire the photons at our metal target.

After shooting a pile of photons, we look at the information collected from the detectors—the toll booths—we placed in front of each slit. What the information from those detectors shows is that indeed each photon behaved just like a particle, no different than a BB, and that each went through only one of the detectors, not both. Now let's take a look at the screen behind the metal. Since we have just done this experiment a few moments earlier, we are certain that we are going to find our old friend, the interference pattern of alternating light and dark lines, indicating the presence of waves that we just saw during the first run of the experiment. But this time that's not what we find. Instead, we find a single line behind each slit, just what we would have expected if we were actually firing BBs through the slit. No interference pattern is seen anywhere, no wave pattern.

We just did the same experiment twice and got completely different results. The only difference between the two experiments is that for the second experiment we placed a detector in front of each slit. For some reason, in this variation of the experiment our photons did not act like waves, but instead acted like particles. Instead of the wave interference pattern of alternating dark and light lines, our screen showed a single line directly behind each slit. The only difference between the first and second experiments is that in the second experiment we "looked"—via our detectors—to see which path the photon took on the way to the screen.

Maybe the detectors were messing things up, so let's run the same experiment a third time. We will keep the detectors in place, but this time we'll turn them off so that we don't get any information from the detectors. When we do that and look at the screen behind the metal, what do we find? Incredibly, we find those alternating light and dark lines again, the interference pattern indicative of a wave. Let's now run the experiment a fourth and final time with the detectors turned on again. What do we find? Once again we lose the wave pattern. All we see is the single line behind each slit, indicating that each photon only went through one slit.

Numerous variations of this experiment have been conducted, some with ingenious methods to try and "fool" the photons, but the result is always the same. If we don't try to detect the path of the photons—no detectors turned on, no way to check them—we get a wave pattern of interference; light is a wave, and each particle travels through both slits, not just one. But look at them as they enter the experiment—observe the path of the photon via the detector—and light is a particle; there is no interference pattern and no wave behavior, just a single line on the screen behind each slit indicating that each photon has chosen a single path. As if this were not sufficiently confusing, a variation of this experiment can be performed where the information about which path the photon took is not obtained until well after the photon has "chosen" to go through one or both slits; the "looking" doesn't occur until long after the photon would have made its choice. If you perform this particular variation of the experiment, the photons will still behave as particles, choosing one slit or the other rather than going through both. It doesn't matter *when* you try to determine the path of the photon, whether before it passes through a slit or long after. The act of "looking" somehow makes the photon act like a particle and forces it to choose a single path. It is equivalent to determining what happened in the past by changing the future!

You have just been introduced to one of the great mysteries of the quantum world: observing an event changes history. It is as if the outcome of a game between two teams changed depending on whether or not anyone watches the contest. Imagine a football game between the Green Bay Packers and the Dallas Cowboys. If the game is not viewed, if the stadium is empty and there is no television broadcast, the Green Bay Packers win. If the stadium is full or if the game is televised, the Dallas Cowboys win. This is the way the quantum world really works. The mere observation of an event changes the outcome; observing actually changes history.

If this were only true of experiments involving photons or electrons, we could easily live with this and move on. But this is not a cartoon;

this is the way the world works, how real events unfold. Something terribly strange is afoot. Why should the mere observance of an event have the ability to change its outcome? And how about those particles that are acting as waves? What's with that? How can a particle act as a wave?

Recall that in the first paragraph of this chapter I mentioned the concept of probability, how quantum physics tells us that we cannot predict with certainty the outcome of any event, only its probability. I'll try to avoid inducing a severe migraine by explaining the physics involved, but it turns out that the location of any particle, like our photon, is never really certain. In fact, our photon is actually more like a probability wave, which I will now explain.

Imagine a very, very large blanket. Take a classroom of preschoolers and have them crawl under this enormous blanket and stand up. Most of the kids will congregate together and create a large "hill" in the middle of the blanket. An occasional child will move away, and we will see a small isolated bump here and there under the blanket as a result. This analogy describes a probability wave for any particle, like our photon. Although it is highly likely we will find a given child near the middle of our blanket, Johnny really could be anywhere, though our odds of finding him decrease as we move farther from the peak of probability. The same is true when we try to predict the exact location of a photon. To add further to the confusion, the "blanket" for our photon is really the entire universe. Quantum physics tells us that our photon, while it is most likely where we expect it to be, could be anywhere in the universe.

Our double-slit and detector experiment demonstrated that our photon, when not being observed, is acting like a very broad probability wave that passes through both slits. Part of the photon's probability wave passes through one slit and part passes through the other, and what we see on the screen is the resulting interference pattern of the two parts of the probability wave colliding with each other. In other words, when we did not attempt to know the precise location of the photon, it really had no position—there was only a probability of places that it *might* be. And since it *might* be anywhere, its probability wave is quite spread out. That is why we saw the interference pattern on the screen, which constitutes proof of the photon's wave-like nature. Once

we turned on the detectors, once we *knew* just where that photon
was, the wave game ended and we had a definite position for the
photon—and therefore we observed the single line of 'hits' on the
screen indicating that discrete particles, not waves, had passed through
the slit.

Particles are probability waves? Hard to believe, but true. Many,
many precise experiments over the past seventy or so years have proved
this to be the way it is. And guess what? We are made of particles; everything in the universe is made of particles that follow these laws of quantum physics. Everything in the world, including you and me, is really a
massive collection of probability waves. We don't perceive this in daily
life because we never find ourselves in a position to notice it: the probability that all of the particles that compose our bodies would suddenly
and simultaneously vanish, only to reappear in another county, is
ridiculously tiny. Nevertheless, it is so.

Back to the problem of observation and its ability to affect the outcome of events. We changed the outcome of our experiment by directly
observing a photon. That photon does not exist as a particle in any one
place until we observe it. What this tells us is that the act of observing
actually creates reality! Photons are real; this is not some game.
Observing events does indeed create different outcomes in the quantum world, which is really our world. Once again, irrefutable proof that
the world is most definitely not what we think! Remember these ideas
about observation and reality, for we will see them again down the road.

Let's add one other patently crazy idea to our current list of bizarre
physics concepts. Another principal of physics is something called *locality*, which simply states that two objects that are separated in space
require some direct interaction between them for one to have an effect
on the other. We *assume* locality. We assume the world is "local," meaning that in order for one object to affect another, something must occur
directly between those two objects. For example, if you and I are separated by one mile and I want you to take the milk out of your refrigerator, I can only get you to do so in a few ways. I could drive over and
ask you face to face. I could call you on the telephone or send you an
email and ask you to get the milk. I could have a skywriter in an air-

plane write the message in the sky. Some action on my part is necessary in order to get you to carry out my request. What I could not do is open the refrigerator in *my* house and take out the milk and expect that in some mysterious way you would then do the same in *your* house.

For one object to have an effect on another, some interaction between the two must take place. Traditional physics, also known as Newtonian physics after the man who uncovered the natural laws of motion, Sir Isaac Newton, states this fact to be true. Einstein added the caveat that whatever interaction or communication takes place between those two objects, it is limited by the speed of light—no signal can surpass that ultimate speed limit.

Turns out that Sir Isaac was not completely correct. (By the way, he was also wrong about time. He described a "clockwork" universe, meaning that the universe was like a clock that had been wound and was just ticking off one moment at a time, at the same rate for each of us. We have already discovered in the last chapter how untrue that turns out to be.) Quantum physics describes a phenomenon called "entanglement," which is when two objects separated by some distance—really any distance, even those enormous light years we discussed previously—become linked in some way, even if they are not in contact with one another. Entanglement leads to some bizarre conclusions. Primarily, it means that the long-standing assumption of locality that we described above is not an accurate representation of how the world works.

We won't spend a great deal of time explaining the physics of this topic, because it is fairly complicated, and because what really matters to us is the result of our inquiry. In nature, tiny particles interact all of the time. Sometimes, as a result of these interactions and processes, two new and identical particles are created. These particles are exact twins, and often they go hurtling off in opposite directions as a result of the process that created them. Since they are usually traveling at the speed of light, it doesn't take long for them to be quite far apart. Yet no matter how far apart they are, if something affects the properties of one of the particles, the other will respond in precisely the same manner as the first. We need an example to illustrate this concept.

Let's assume that two twin boys, Steve and Sam, take two different vacations at the same time. Sam visits their maternal grandpa in California; Steve visits their paternal grandpa in New York. Imagine that a game of "Simon Says" is taking place at each grandparent's home at the exact same time—except that only the California grandpa is calling out the instructions; the grandpa in New York is silent. No telephone or email or any other form of communication exists between the two households. Grandpa in California looks at Sam and says, "Simon says stand on your right foot." Sam complies and stands on his right foot. At the exact same moment, three thousand miles away, Steve stands on his right foot. California grandpa then says, "Simon says touch your nose with your left thumb." Again, Sam follows the instructions, and at the exact same moment Steve does the same in New York, although no one told him to do so. Remember, there is no communication between the two households, and no time elapses between Sam's actions and Steve's.

Sam and Steve are "entangled." For some mysterious reason that flies in the face of both Sir Isaac Newton and even Albert Einstein (since the response of the entangled particles, or people in this case, is far faster than the speed of light, and Einstein insisted that no interaction could exceed that limit), entangled particles always react in precisely the same way to any event. What's more—and this is something that has been repeatedly proven by very sophisticated experiments over the past thirty years—this has nothing to do with the particles being pre-programmed. No pre-set code exists in each that predicts their behavior. No matter what random action is taken, these entangled particles will always react in precisely the same way, no matter their location and no matter how great their separation. Such behavior is not only remarkable, but it shows complete contempt for logic and for the laws of physics that have proven so dependable for hundreds of years. Frankly, it is nothing short of magic. But it is all true, and has been proven many times over by precise and exacting experiments.

What is the significance of entangled particles? For our purposes, it is merely to demonstrate that interactions occur in our world which are not only unexpected but which completely fracture our common understanding of how the world works. Before the discovery of quantum physics, we would never have imagined that objects separated in space could possibly demonstrate such behavior. As we mentioned, locality was just assumed—just as the non-changing nature of space and time were assumed.

Let's summarize what we have discovered in these last two chapters:

(1) Time is not what we have always imagined. All moments are coexistent——past, present and future——and no one moment is more "alive" than another.

(2) "Now" is not the same for all of us. In fact, my now and your now may be different. The greater the distance between us, and/or the greater the difference in our speed relative to each other, the greater the disparity between our nows.

(3) Time passes more slowly the faster you travel. One will age far less while traveling at super speeds in comparison to one who is not traveling at such speeds.

(4) There is a limit to how fast we can go, and that limit is the speed of light. No matter how hard you try, you can never exceed that limit.

(5) Objects don't have finite locations, only probabilities of existing in one location or another. When we attempt to observe the location of an object, only then does it have a precise location. The act of observing changes the outcome; the act of observing creates reality! A photon acts as a wave when no one is looking and as a particle when observed.

(6) Crazy and impossible as it may seem, the future can affect the present, or the past. In the experiment in which we determined the path of a photon using our detectors——our toll booths——the photon acted as a particle, even when we measured its path retroactively. An observation made in the particle's future determined its action in the present, forcing it to act in a particle-like way rather than in a wave-like way. As if it knew we would be watching.

(7) "Entanglement" refers to the idea that two objects can be mysteriously related such that they respond simultaneously to any singular event, even if separated by enormous distances. This concept upends conventional physics, since there should be no way that the two objects can behave in this way if the standard laws of the universe as we have come to accept them are correct.

Quantum physics is about the very small. It describes the behavior of particles too miniscule to see. Similarly, Einstein's theory of special relativity only becomes obvious at extreme rates of speed. Existing as we do in our "large" world of objects and in our relatively slow world of motion, we don't notice quantum physics and relativity. But they are real nonetheless, and they are frankly nothing less than wild and bizarre. Who could seriously imagine that our perception of time's steady flow is an illusion? How incredible is it that yesterday and tomorrow are every bit as alive as today? Is it not amazing that the act of observing an event can change its outcome?

You may have found some of these concepts difficult to follow. They are difficult to follow! Whether or not you understand every nuance of relativity and quantum physics is not important for our purposes. The conclusion that relativity and quantum physics forces upon us is this: there are things that we have always taken for granted in the physical world—the constancy of time and space; the separation of past, present, and future; and the certainty of events—which are false. Time and space are not the simple constants we have assumed them to be. Past, present, and future, as Einstein himself stated, are an illusion. There is no certainty in this world, only probability. We have no other option— we are forced to agree that the world is indeed not what we think. And that has huge implications for every facet of our lives, as we shall see as we move ahead.

chapter six

THE SOFTER CLUES

We have just spent the past two chapters exploring the physical world. We found that the world we thought we knew so well was full of surprises. Although our exploration of time, space, and the quantum world was a bit confusing, at least these are subjects that can be examined and verified by experimentation. We were able to show that what seemed so bizarre was nonetheless true. We uncovered troubling but hard facts.

Now we are going to move away from the purely physical to explore those clues, offered up to us on a regular basis, that are not founded in hard science. The softer clues that we will discuss are another manifestation of our incomplete knowledge of reality. What do I mean by that? We assume that what we see is what we get. We trust our senses; we trust what we can see and touch. The strangeness of the quantum world and the bizarre nature of time prove to us beyond a shadow of a doubt that our senses mislead us, that in fact what we see is only a small part of what is true. We operate with incomplete information.

A young child is familiar with but one world, that of her family. As far as she knows, everyone in the world eats dinner at six o'clock when Dad and Mom return from work. Everyone drinks milk for breakfast but not for dinner. Everyone always butters both sides of the bread. According to the information available to her, that is just how the world is.

Since she is in the house every evening before six, she has no idea that when the weather is not inclement a few girls her age in her neighborhood play a game of tag in the park at six o'clock. She has no idea that some people drink wine for dinner or that jam is preferred to butter by over a billion people. For that child, this is information not yet available, so her conclusions about how life should be lived are severely limited. She acts the way she does because it is what is done in the only world she knows.

So it is with all of us. Child or adult, our knowledge is limited, and therefore our potential approaches to the world are also necessarily limited. So much more exists beneath the veneer than we can appreciate through our senses, and our survey from chapter three indicates that most of us share this conclusion. As we investigate and question, we uncover additional clues about the nature of the world. Each clue we uncover helps us complete our picture of reality. Until we reach a full and true understanding of our reality, we will be operating with incomplete information, just like our young child above. And therefore, as with her, our decisions about how to approach our lives and how to interact with each other are likely to be suboptimal.

We begin with this statement that I present to you. *Life cannot possibly be what we think it is.*

Take a moment and remove yourself from the world. Senseless tragedies occur on a daily basis, from the terminal illness of a young child to large-scale death and destruction by the hand of either man or Mother Nature. We accept tragedy as part of the world, just as we accept snow in the winter in the northern hemisphere and daily precipitation in the rainy season in tropical climates. We accept these as a given: that's just the way our world works. But that's not necessarily the only way the world could be. For example, our world could just as easily have been created so that it snowed in the tropics. Sound crazy? Only if you assume that just one set of chemical laws and one set of physical laws are possible. As I mentioned earlier, such an assumption is naïve. For centuries man believed that the earth was the center of the universe, and some who questioned that belief—some who thought *that* concept naïve—were persecuted and murdered for their heresy.

Our world need not be as it is; other permutations are possible. For example, our world could have been created without tragedies. Childhood cancers and fatal accidents need not be natural, inevitable.

Brutality and repression, earthquakes and tornadoes—all of the horrors that we accept as "normal" are components of just one possible reality among many. But saying so, of course, does not make it true; we need to investigate further in order to prove this unusual notion.

Recall from the last chapter on quantum physics that all events are initially, before they happen, merely probabilities. A universe could exist (and indeed might: a good many serious physicists assume that an infinite number of universes exist) where none of these sorrowful events occur. This is not wild-eyed speculation. Indeed, it is a logical deduction from what we have already learned from quantum physics. The fact that our world is constructed as it is and has the laws that it does is an important clue to our purpose here in this life, in this world. Once you understand that our world is not "just the way it is" by accident but is instead just one possibility among many, then it begins to seem less likely that we find ourselves in this universe, in this permutation, by accident or at random.

It is well known that the physical world is incredibly fine-tuned. If any one of just a few physical factors were even a hair different, life could not exist on this earth. If the percentage of oxygen making up the air were off just a bit, the cellular processes required for life would not be possible. If water were most dense at zero degrees Celsius instead of four degrees—which is true for all other liquids—then lakes and rivers would freeze from the bottom up. This would be catastrophic, not only for fish that obviously could not survive inside a block of ice. The entire ecosystem of our planet would be radically altered, eventually eliminating life. If the nuclear forces within the atom—the energy that holds protons and neutrons together within the atom— were just a smidge different, matter would not be possible. Atoms would either fly apart or come crashing in on themselves. Gravity, something we all depend on, is just right for life on Earth; any stronger or weaker and chaos would ensue. Imagine trying to walk on Jupiter where gravity is over twice what it is on Earth. A man weighing 170 pounds on Earth would weigh over 400 pounds on Jupiter. Not only ambulation would be affected: all of our bodily functions would be challenged.

Our world is incredibly "definite." The way all of the pieces fit together is incredibly precise. For centuries, many have claimed that such precision implies the existence of a deity, that there is a grand design. Such a claim, even if perfectly true, does not disprove science. The two are not only compatible but logical. A grand designer would likely create a self-perpetuating system that provides consistent results; we might term this science. Even in our impressive technological world, however, there are those who still dispute science—particularly evolution. The substitution of myth for science is foolish, but I find this substitution distressing primarily because it avoids the larger, more important question. That question is not whether or not a deity exists and is responsible for this universe, but rather this: for what reason was our world constructed in this precise and unique way?

Some would argue that this point of view is fallacious. Our universe is the way it is because it is the *only way* it could be. If it weren't this way, the argument goes, there would be no life at all. We are actually living in the one universe where life as we know it is possible, where all of the physical factors we mentioned above are exactly as they need to be; other possible universes with slightly different physical laws wouldn't work.

If you took the New York City telephone book, cut it up into the individual eight million entries, took those entries and put them in a huge bag, shook up the bag, dragged it up to the top of the Empire State Building, opened it, and dropped all of the pieces onto the pavement below and repeated this process a trillion trillion trillion times or so, on one of those trillion trillion trillion drops all of the words would fall into the correct order, reconstituting the original phone book. Quantum physics teaches us that this is a reasonable conclusion. (Disclosure: this is not a universally-agreed-on principle—there are some physicists who would disagree.) If after reading this book you wish to believe that this is what our universe represents—essentially the perfect, random reconstitution of the New York City telephone book—there is not much I can do to prove you wrong. For me, considering what we have learned about the way the world works, it's a bit of a stretch.

If the world is not random—and I do believe that the precision of the physical world and the many other clues we will identify in this book argue strongly against our world being random—then it is legitimate to infer a purpose, and that has critical implications for us humans. The fact that our world is constructed as it is—not just in terms of physical properties, but also because it allows for both horrific tragedies and unlimited amounts of joy—is an enormous clue. It doesn't have to be this way; quantum physics proves that it is but one possibility out of an infinite number of possibilities. But it *is* this way, this precise, particular way. SOMETHING IS GOING ON HERE.

We repeat history on both a personal and a community level. Each of us makes the same mistakes as those who preceded us. Nations rise and fall as they have for all of recorded history. Nothing really ever changes. While we are in the midst of this chaos, while we pursue the daily responsibilities that occupy our time and our minds, we don't take notice of this state of affairs. It is only when we reflect on the entirety of the world that we begin to realize that the whole thing is a bit weird. Why don't we really learn from our mistakes? Why does generation after generation experience the same trials and tribulations? Why don't we progress to a higher life form, one that does not build and create only to then destroy? Once again, SOMETHING IS GOING ON HERE.

Ontogeny recapitulates phylogeny. This quite technical piece of verbiage, coined in the nineteenth century, means that the embryologic development of a human fetus mirrors the overall evolution of the animal kingdom. Just as the animal kingdom radiated outward—beginning with the earliest life forms and then elaborating upon these forms until complicated vertebrates appeared—a human embryo, it was said, proceeded through the same stages that the animal kingdom as a whole did as it moved from primitive algae to fish, to amphibians, and finally to apes and humans. The idea is not true. Nature does not really work this way. Human embryos don't look like fish and then reptiles on their way to becoming primates. But there is nevertheless an important metaphor here.

Our collective life in our communities and in society mirrors our individual progression. Life is nothing but repetitious. For humans, learning never ends; we continue to grow and mature for decades. Infants are helpless. As young children we test and experiment in order to learn our way around our small universe. Even adults are continually learning—we learn not only the facts of our existence but also how to relate to one another and to successfully function in changing environments. In our later years we begin to deteriorate, to lose the skills we worked so hard to learn over all of those decades.

Societies and entire civilizations behave in a similar manner. In their early stages, they too experiment in order to find the common ground that will allow the group to survive and then hopefully thrive. Unfortunately, history has also demonstrated the inevitable demise of civilizations. The end has not come in the same manner or for the same reasons each time, but no society has lasted unchanged for a millenium. That may sound like a long time, but when the denominator is 100,000 to 200,000 years it's hardly a fraction worth mentioning.

This transience of human life and of human societies and cultures is no accident. The play gets re-written and re-performed over and over and over again. We take this for granted, but upon reflection it seems odd. We don't seem to collectively learn anything; we don't seem to collectively accrue wisdom. Darwinian evolution is established fact. Species adapt or perish. New life forms evolve from less efficient models. But it is not clear that the human world operates in the same manner.

An endless repetitive cycle occurs with remarkably little if any progress. While it is true that I am writing this book on a computer with highly sophisticated word processing software rather than on parchment, this is not as significant an advancement as it might seem. I am writing about the same issues that have plagued mankind since humans arrived on this planet. Impressive advancement would be an absence of conflict between cultures and nations, the defeat of tyranny and injustice, and the end of violence among men. But these remain as much a part of our world as they were centuries ago. Genuine advancement would mean evolving into a higher life form; we have not, and there is no evidence that we're headed that way. Once again we uncover a clue: SOMETHING IS GOING ON HERE.

Aging presents another clue. Our personal perspective is perpetually in flux. Recall how, when you were in kindergarten at age five, those sixth graders you watched in the school hallways seemed so mature and worldly. As a teenager you assumed a thirty-year-old was completely grown up, while that same thirty-year-old was still trying to make sense of family and career and wondering what he would be when he really grew up.

Someone in his sixties has difficulty guessing the age of a young person; is he twenty-five or thirty-five? Someone in that twenty-something age group could probably state the age of another in his generation within a year of accuracy. We can be even more graphic. An adolescent boy can always identify a girl of his age, while his father probably could only guess her age within a three-year range, if that. Dad would also be much more focused on the good-looking mother of his son's girlfriend than the fifteen-year-old girlfriend (let's ignore the occasional pathology for now). Just natural, you would say, but why? Why do the things that interest and attract us change as we age? Why should our adolescent boy prefer his classmate, and why should his father prefer her mother? Such a question seems foolish; of course we change. But just why we change is not so clear. It could just as easily be the other way around. Our interests and our perspective could remain fixed once established, but they don't. Why is that? We evolve, you might answer. Indeed we do, but then again, why? Why bother? What's the advantage?

You might respond that it's just part of the process of aging, but that generates another question: what is aging? Recall from our discussion of Einstein and relativity that all moments in time are real. Past, present, and future hold no special place in the loaf of bread that is space-time; they all exist forever. Our childhoods are as alive as our twilight years. What is this phenomenon that seems to move us from one state of mind to the next, from adolescent to young adult to elderly? At my twentieth high-school reunion, I saw friends I had not seen since we were teenagers. Here is the thought that filled my mind as I watched them enter the room: why are my friends wearing their parents' clothing? I was at that moment the teenager from high school, not the almost-forty-year-old. Feelings and thoughts I had abandoned, or that had abandoned me years before, were right back in my consciousness. After an hour or so of catching up with some of these people and recounting my experiences of the prior twenty years, I was back in my current "now," no longer a high school student. There is no question in my mind that I had temporarily slid back along that timeline and revisited the past for that short interval.

We assume the changes of aging, just as we assume so many facets of our lives. These things just are; it's the way of the world. But as I hope you are beginning to appreciate, that is an insufficient answer. Remember, our world is but one potential world out of an infinite number of possible worlds.

The human body is composed of trillions of cells. The behavior and the longevity of our cells are the result of software—our DNA, which is programmed to allow only a finite existence for each cell. Some cells live a long time, some for a brief time. The entire organism, however, is programmed for a limited existence. The length of this existence can be altered both positively and negatively. Good nutrition and avoiding danger add to its length; disease and accidents detract. No matter how careful we are, eventually the organism will cease to function—we will die.

But the organism, the human, need not be programmed for aging and cell death. Our cells could have been programmed to divide and grow limitlessly. We only age because that's what the DNA says to do, because our software determines our fate. It is not hard to imagine that the program, our DNA, could be written in a different manner, just as any software can be modified. If our DNA code were written differently, cells would not age, nor would we. Our existence would go from finite to infinite.

I am not making the case to re-engineer our genome, the code of our DNA, to promote eternal life. The point is that the way we are programmed is no accident. It could have been that we were programmed for non-obsolescence, so that the cells that compose our organs would replicate and rejuvenate perpetually, the next generation a precise copy of the previous. Our bodies could have been programmed to identify and repair every mutation, or a kind of mutation-proof DNA could have arisen instead. We would then never age, not a single cell. We would never change. Our brain cells would be constant, just as our skin and our heart cells would be. Our likes and dislikes would be set, our personalities fixed, our knowledge frozen.

We might wonder whether that would be a good thing or a bad thing. That is not the point. The point is that this is not the way it is. This is a blindingly bright clue to the nature of our reality. The fact that we do age—and that our interests, our perspectives, and our knowledge change over time—is a powerful indication of purpose, not randomness. Let's explore this further.

Humans have an enormous capacity to learn, far beyond the capabilities of any other animal. Other animals quickly learn to seek food and shelter, to care for their young, to avoid predators, and, depending on the species, to form communities for protection and the acquisition of basic needs. They don't build ever more ingenious structures, uncover mathematical and scientific truths, or write poetry. They are born, they relatively rapidly reach their potential, and then they survive as best they can for as long as they can.

We are clearly quite different. We mature incredibly slowly. We advance in our physical abilities over an extended period of time, and in our mental skills over an even longer period. We in fact never stop learning. So the question is, why? Why do we continue to learn, and why do we learn at all? Once we have achieved the ability to feed, shelter, clothe, and protect ourselves and our loved ones, why do we continue to learn? We know that we are no different than the remainder of the earth's animals in that our time is limited. We will die. So why does our learning continue right up until the end?

As we age most of us mature. We become far more comfortable in our own skin. We worry less about what others think of us. We become more patient. We better understand the nuances of life. Where is the survival advantage in this? We would be far better off as individuals if we learned these things much earlier in life, or better yet if they were programmed into our brains from the beginning. More patience would certainly be a good thing. We would drive more slowly and have fewer accidents: 80 percent of auto accidents in the U.S. involve drivers under the age of twenty-five. Most violent crimes are committed by the young. If we were wiser and more patient at a far earlier age, we would certainly be less violent, which by itself would increase the longevity of others and ourselves. Fatal accidents of all types are far less common among the more mature.

The fact that we learn so slowly appears to be a handicap for our species. No doubt, as a singular factor in survival, we would fare better if we had evolved to be more knowledgeable in our younger years. Of course this is not the way it is. We do learn incrementally, from toddlerhood through our advanced years, and only dementia places any limit on our ability to learn right through to the end. In fact we are, in the most important areas, wisest at or near the end. This is a curious phenomenon that on the surface appears to be a great waste. If the goal of life is merely to survive as long as possible, as it appears to be for the rest of the animal kingdom, then something is amiss. Knowledge and certainly wisdom would be most beneficial to us in our early years when we have the most to gain and the most to lose, and their value would diminish with time.

We must then ask why this is not the case. Why do we learn incrementally over eighty years? We all make errors, more of them when we are young. The errors you have made in your life are probably not too dissimilar from those made by your parents and grandparents and by others in generations past. This is another curiosity. It would seem that we should collectively learn to avoid these mistakes as we evolve, but we don't. Each of us seems "required" to repeat the mistakes of our ancestors.

In my previous book, *What Do I Do Now? A Handbook for Life*, I spent an entire chapter on what I termed "dumb moves." Dumb moves are those errors that lead either to serious injury or death, or in some way create at least semi-permanent havoc in your life. One could conclude that we should have evolved in such a way as to avoid dumb moves, since these clearly lead to a shorter period of survival. In fact, one could also assume that those genes that make us less intelligent and prone to make dumb moves would be selected out of the genome. Ignorance is quite detrimental to success and survival, while intelligence should deliver greater yields of both. We seem collectively no smarter than we were ten thousand years ago.

We could have been programmed differently. Intelligence could have had more of an impact on human evolution than it seems to have had. We need not have been constructed in this way, destined to repeat those same dumb moves generation after generation. As an example, let's take war. In the short term, war occasionally makes a difference, but never in the long term. The victors are victors temporarily; no culture or nation reigns forever. We kill thousands, yet benefit from no long-term gain. We still assume that one culture, one religion, one *opinion* should prevail, while the story of the world proves the opposite. Where is the evolved brain in this scenario?

Serious students of evolution would be quick to jump on the assertion that intelligence should be a selected trait as humans evolve. Theories exist that claim that it is not the species, nor even the individual, that strives to survive and multiply—the unit of evolution is the gene (Richard Dawkins—*The Selfish Gene*). Very intelligent and less intelligent humans mate for many reasons; intelligence is not a single trait to be passed on from generation to generation.

It is not my intention in this book to argue opposing theories of evolution, and certainly not to in any way diminish the proven facts about evolution. I have included this brief discussion of evolution solely as one additional soft clue we may employ to solve the greater puzzle— why are we humans here in the first place?

Wars, prejudice, and the desire for power all create waves of death and destruction and never yield a different world. No other fact is more apparent when we examine history, yet we never, ever change. Once again, it could have been different. We could have been programmed to assimilate this information, to actually learn and to become smarter, but we were not. Even in this era of amazing technology, we are no different than generations past.

Even if we have not evolved as expected, as a species, what about the evolution of our individual lives? While it would be preferable to be born much smarter, or at least to learn the maximum at the earliest possible age, neither is the case. We have an incredible capacity to learn, especially in our younger years, so although we are born with suboptimal knowledge, surely we could absorb this information rapidly and efficiently. Turns out that hasn't worked so well either. In fact, teaching life's lessons to the young—lessons that are required if the child is to avoid dumb moves and if he or she is to maximize the potential for a rich, full, and long life—is quite difficult. Adolescents, those who would most benefit from this kind of information, are the most resistant to that information. Doesn't that seem odd in terms of survival advantage? Adolescents should be the most hungry for such information, not the least. How do we explain this phenomenon?

Clearly there is something critical about learning on our own, through our own experiences. If that were not the case, we would need only to read self-help books beginning in kindergarten, and by fifteen we would be all set and ready to go. But as adolescents, we assume life will go on forever. There is no sense of urgency to achieve or to learn; the future is interminable. And so we set off on courses filled with danger while simultaneously missing opportunities that could markedly increase the probability of our prolonged survival and of a more successful existence.

Why must we learn on our own? Many men (and some women) are loath to ask for directions while traveling, insisting on figuring it out for themselves. I have always found this to be curious. Why would you struggle to decipher a route when in two seconds a knowledgeable person could provide the answer? Clearly the knowledge gained from experience differs from that provided by the written or spoken word. Everyone knows this; it is no great revelation. But *why* is this so? If the goal of life is only maximum longevity, then we would be far better served if we did the opposite and learned what we needed to know in easier ways, ways that didn't involve experiment and failure. Learning by experience takes a great deal of time and is fraught with potential danger, both of which lead to diminished longevity.

Human life seems backwards. Conventional thinking, if not evolutionary theory, assumes that we humans are striving for maximum longevity. While the advent of sanitation, advanced medicines, and other scientific and technological discoveries has lengthened the average life span—at least in first-world countries—our human nature has not contributed to this advantage. We begin life in a helpless state and remain frighteningly so for many years. We are most wise when it is least advantageous (during our later years), and relatively ignorant when it matters most.

A reasonable conclusion from this discussion—one in line with the theory that it is the perpetuation of genes, not individuals, that is paramount in evolution—is that maximum longevity is not the goal of human life.

Everyone who has ever driven a car has had the following experience. You are on a long trip, cruising down the highway at the speed limit. You suddenly notice that the mile marker indicates that you just covered twenty miles in what seemed like an instant. You have no recollection of those past twenty miles, no recollection of the scenery, the cars passed, or even the thoughts that occupied your mind during that time. You didn't veer off the road or crash the car; all is well. But those twenty miles and those twenty minutes are a blank.

Sometimes other parts of your life are similar. You took on a project, or overcame some adversity, or developed an idea. In retrospect, you have no understanding of how you succeeded or how the idea arose. Suddenly something quite significant is accomplished, twenty miles worth of ideas and effort, and you have no earthly idea how it happened.

Such gaps in subjective time are universal, but we make little of this phenomenon. It's no big deal, just another one of life's curiosities. Except that it *does* happen, to everyone, and it is nothing short of amazing. We do things we cannot explain. "Where did that poem or that song come from? It just sort of showed up in my consciousness." Or, "How did I successfully just deal with that terrifying experience? I never knew I had it in me." It's sort of magic when these things occur. We can't explain them except to say that we just have more in us than we assumed. Since it is ubiquitous in humans, it's just part of what makes us tick. Right, and that's the point. There is a great deal about us that is not so easily explained.

I began this section by stating that *life cannot possibly be what we think it is.* As we have seen, the progression of our collective history and of our individual lives is contrary to much of what we would expect to see in a world that is primarily random. Our world is just one world out of perhaps an infinite number of permutations of worlds; it is exceedingly specific.

We take so many things for granted. It is only when we stop and contemplate the mundane and accepted that we have the opportunity to explore these assumptions. Why do we age as we do? Why do our perspectives subtly evolve almost imperceptibly? Why do we repeat the same mistakes as all those who came before? Why isn't wisdom cumulative, easily passed from one generation to the next so that the same mistakes can be avoided? To assume randomness lurking here—to assume that it's just the way it is—is just as naïve as to assume that the percentage of oxygen in the air or the force of gravity or the attractive forces between the particles in the nucleus of an atom are just random scientific facts. Collectively, these are clues. They point us to the conclusion that the world is not what we think. Which brings us to the nature of reality.

chapter seven

REALITY

R eality is one of those concepts that doesn't seem to require much
analysis. Reality just is. Each morning we awaken and find ourselves immersed in it. Reality is something shared by all, an
enormous happening in which everyone participates. While our individual experiences will vary, they seem to occur within a universal and
singular framework.

Recall from our discussion of Einstein and relativity that if two people are in motion relative to each other, their clocks will not be synchronized—their "nows" are different, and time passes at a different
rate for each of them. While this is peculiar, we don't make much of this
in our daily lives, because the difference in our respective speeds is very,
very small. Nonetheless, as soon as we accept that nows can be different, we are confirming that the assumption of a universal and singular
reality is flawed. Extending the idea at the heart of relativity, we can say
that our notion of what is real and true cannot be an absolute: our
neighbor can have a different perception or a different set of measure-
ments. Reality becomes quite personal, something that is truly in the
eye of the beholder. Because if these physical and measurable discrep-
ancies happen at all—and relativity shows that they do, even if we do
not encounter them in our daily lives—then it means something larger.
The effects of relativity mean that we hold an assumption about reality that is not true. This is important because we each are constantly
creating realities, and this is nothing short of amazing.

"We create reality? Are you kidding? But I'm constantly battling reality, trying to survive reality, hoping reality doesn't swallow me whole!"

That is certainly the impression life forces upon us. Reality happens, and then we sink or swim. We seem to be, if not victims, then certainly pawns in the game of reality. But once again, the world is not what it appears to be. It is in fact just the converse: we each create reality, all of it.

Franklin, a manager for a consulting company, is about to leave his office in Philadelphia at the end of the workday. His parking garage is to his right as he exits his building, but just as he walks through the glass front door he recalls that he ran out of shaving cream this morning. The pharmacy is one block to his left, in the opposite direction of his parked car. Franklin pauses. "Do I have time to run to the pharmacy before heading home?" He recalls that a contractor is coming to his house tonight to discuss a home improvement project he and his wife are planning. "If I hurry," he decides, "I can make it."

So Franklin turns to his left towards the pharmacy. He begins to jog. The pharmacy is on the other side of the street, and the light is red in that direction, forcing him to stop. Just as he reaches the corner, he stumbles and inadvertently knocks over an elderly woman who was waiting for the light to change before crossing. Franklin picks himself up and rushes over to her; it is immediately evident that she is hurt. "My hip," she moans. "I think I broke my hip." Soon the paramedics arrive, and indeed the woman has broken her hip.

The woman's only daughter lives across the country in Sacramento, California. She is married and has two children, a boy fourteen and a daughter age nine. Her husband works for the county government as a supervisor. When the daughter hears of her mother's accident that evening, she decides she must travel to Philadelphia to assist, and she leaves the following morning. That evening, since his mother is gone, the fourteen-year-old son decides to help out his dad and make dinner for the three of them. He knows how to boil water to make spaghetti, so before his dad returns from work he puts a pot of water on the cook top and turns on the gas. Unfortunately, he does not notice the dish-towel next to the burner, and a fire begins. The son thinks quickly, calls 911 and then hangs up and beats the flames back. The fire department soon arrives, but the fire is already out and no injuries are sustained.

The father returns from work. He is of course relieved that his children are unharmed and that the fire caused minimal damage. As he turns to thank the firemen, he recognizes one of the firemen as his classmate from high school, whom he has not seen in years. The two talk briefly and decide to meet for dinner the following week.

Seven days later, the fireman is on his way to the restaurant to meet his old friend. He finds street parking two blocks from the restaurant and begins his walk. Out of the corner of his eye he notices smoke seeping from the window of a row house. He rushes across the street, forces open the door, enters the house, and finds a four-year-old girl huddled under the kitchen table, trembling and in tears as the fire rages only feet away. The fireman grabs the girl, carries her out of the house, and rushes back in to save the girl's mother who is unconscious on the second floor. Mother and daughter are safe, and they recover completely.

Our young girl grows up, gets a doctorate in pharmacology, and thirty-five years later to the day from the evening of the fire, she invents a drug that prevents malaria. Millions of people worldwide, mostly children, are saved from this devastating disease.

If Franklin had chosen to wait until the next day to buy his shaving cream instead of getting it that evening, he would have turned right as he exited his workplace instead of left towards the pharmacy. The elderly woman would have safely crossed the street, and her daughter would have remained in Sacramento and prepared dinner for her children the following night. No fire would have ensued; no reunion between a husband and an old classmate would have been planned. A fireman would not have parked his car near a burning house, and no one would have saved a young girl from the fire in her home.

You don't believe that we each continually create reality?

Of course it is possible that someone else would have passed that house that evening and noticed the fire. Perhaps the girl would eventually have run out of the house on her own. If not, someone else could have invented the drug that prevented malaria. We don't know. What we do know is that we each make choices, collectively billions of choices on a daily basis, and each and every one has repercussions. Every single action has consequences. Most perhaps are not as significant in their effects as are the ones in our hypothetical tale, but many are. Each one sets off a chain reaction of additional actions, like the story of the butterfly that flaps its wings and initiates the cascade of events that results in a devastating storm down the road of space and time. This is how the world works. There are no meaningless choices; every choice we make has an effect somewhere at some time.

If presented with a choice of A or B or C, we contemplate the pros and cons of each and make a decision. We assume a hierarchy; one of the choices must be the best of the three. But is that really the case? Among A, B, and C, is there really a "best" choice? Consider this question in the context of our friend Franklin who chose to turn left towards the pharmacy instead of right towards his car. He was presented with two options, and in choosing one or the other he was selecting one of two future realities. We know the events that stemmed from his "left turn" choice, but we have no idea about the reality that he would have created had he turned right instead. That "right turn" reality may have meant life or death for someone else, perhaps even for Franklin. We cannot possibly know the long-term consequences of the choices we make, and since those consequences are unknowable, there is no way to rate them in order of preference. Each choice spawns its own reality, its own cascade of events. In turn, each resulting event creates its own cascade of additional events. That assumption—that of several choices one is best—is completely destroyed when we understand how reality is created. There cannot possibly be a "best" choice.

Recall for a moment the photon from our discussion of quantum physics. An infinite number of paths are available to that photon. Only when we try to discern its location does it make its choice. All of the available paths represent legitimate options for that photon; none is preferable over another. So it is with our choices in life. Each one offers a legitimate path and confers a specific consequence or series of consequences; each one delivers a unique reality. *No one reality is more preferred or more special than another; they are all equivalent options.*

What I am implying is that there is no "best" sequence of events, no best choice. But that flies in the face of reason. Surely from our human perspective there are preferred outcomes. Some choices bring justice and joy, others oppression and misery. Some choices prolong or improve life, others shorten or destroy it. Why should I convince my children to work hard in school if I believe that all possible outcomes for their future are equivalent? Doesn't that imply that a beggar or a thief is the equal of a Nobel laureate or a saint?

From the viewpoint of the universe, there is in fact no "best" choice. It is harsh, it is unsettling, but it is nevertheless true. The universe is indifferent to our personal choices. No choice, from the universe's perspective, is more favored or more preferable than another. Clearly our choices are anything but irrelevant to us personally. Who would not rather live free than oppressed? Who would choose hunger over a full stomach? Who would choose poverty over comfort? Our choices matter a great deal to us during our lives, but from the vantage point of the universe, one choice is no more special or desirable than another.

The point I am making is that in the totality of life, all options are equal and available; all will create *some* reality. Have you ever wondered, "What if I choose to do A instead of B?" where A is the daring choice and B the safe, conservative choice? You know that choosing A is risky and a bit crazy. In fact, you know that you should absolutely choose B, but you are enticed by that bit of craziness. You know that A will create an uncertain reality and that all hell may break loose if even the slightest twist occurs.

What if A makes you ill or hurts someone else? What if A ruins your life? Does the universe really care that you chose A? Once again we must view this from two frames of reference. If you choose A and something bad happens to you, it is a certainty that as a consequence of your choice, and the ensuing cascade of events that follow from your choice, something good will happen to someone else. For example, you have two job offers. Offer B is for a rather mundane but secure job. Offer A is for a sexier and more exciting job, but the company is a bit shaky. You choose A, the sexier job. Company B, the safer and more boring company, hires someone else instead of you. Two months later, Company A goes out of business and you are once again unemployed. From your frame of reference, choosing the riskier job turns out to have been an unwise decision, but from the frame of reference of that person who got the secure job with Company B, your choice was a godsend.

Your choice of the riskier Company A created a different reality than would have been the case if you had chosen the safer job with Company B. This reality is detrimental to you, but it greatly benefited that other individual, for whom your choice was a blessing. So was your choice of the riskier job over the safer job a good decision? For you clearly not, but for that other someone clearly yes. And that is how it is with every choice or decision we make. Reality is created, and it is a mix of good and bad, always a mix of rising and sinking fortunes. Good and bad don't factor into the equation since they cancel out. Choice equals reality; there are no adjectives or modifiers in this equation. The universe unfolds in different ways depending on our choices, but it always unfolds; it cannot be stopped. Reality has no net worth; it just is.

We are all aware that there is a balance in nature. Specific events do shift the balance one way or another and often create a state of disorder. But no matter the magnitude of the event, a correction will always follow, and eventually the system will be in equilibrium again. The period of correction may be short or exceedingly long, but there is always a return to balance. Months after a devastating forest fire, new growth is visible on the forest floor. Countless animals may have perished during the blaze, but nature moves along, re-creating life and rebalancing the ecosphere as if nothing had happened. No matter the degree of catastrophe, there is always the movement towards a new equilibrium.

Some may think that the term "equilibrium" means a return to order, but this is incorrect. Equilibrium implies a return to a lower energy state, and this lower energy state does not mean a state of order. In fact, it signifies the converse. It takes energy to create order. Consider a bowl of soup that you place in the microwave oven to heat. You exert energy to place it in the oven, and then you must utilize electrical energy to get the microwave to heat the soup. Once the microwave finishes, you remove the soup, but just as you are about to enjoy it you receive an important telephone call. Ten minutes later, you have concluded your call only to find that your soup is no longer hot. Those heated-up molecules in your soup have interacted with the colder air molecules above the soup and have transferred heat to them. Now the previously cool air molecules are a bit warmer, and the soup colder. Equilibrium has been restored, but you have a cold bowl of soup. You expended energy to heat up that soup, and now all of your work has been wasted. You wished to create a definite order of things—hot soup, cold air— and instead got a disappointing disorder, equilibrium.

As our lives ebb and flow, we witness this sequence in our own lives. Always, there is a recalibration after any event. Always, we tend towards equilibrium. Once again, we must ask why this is so. Recall from our earlier discussion that the possibilities for the nature of the world are infinite, and our specific world is a manifestation of but one possible combination. We assume that there will be a natural tendency to return to equilibrium, since that is what we have always experienced in our world. But it need not be so. Our world could have been constructed so that there would be no natural return to equilibrium. We could live in a world where it is natural to swing far off the midline and never return to a state of balance. But we don't; that's not how our particular world is. In our world, systems tend to seek equilibrium. More correctly, they seek to maximize something called entropy.

Entropy, a rather complicated topic, refers to the relative state of order versus disorder in a system. Maximum disorder is maximum entropy, and vice versa. Your teenager's room, if unattended by a parent, will move from order—clothes in drawers—to less order—clothes strewn throughout the room, increasing the total entropy. Nature prefers disorder; nature encourages maximum entropy. In fact, it takes quite a bit of energy to move from less order to more order: picking up and folding all of those randomly distributed clothes takes work. It's not easy to clean up a mess.

So why the preference for maximizing entropy? Why is our world constructed to require so much effort to keep things neatly sorted? Why this urge to move towards equilibrium—our soup cooling off instead of staying forever hot—which in effect means the maximization of disorder? Most of us prefer order to disorder. A billion dollar industry exists just to provide containers for us to sort our belongings, to keep our personal worlds tidy. Yet the universe is just the opposite; the more disorder the better. Ever get the feeling that some days you are swimming upstream against the current? Well, you are, and not some days but *every* day. We live in a world where disorder is not only the natural state of affairs, but one which demands that we continually and perpetually maintain our efforts to create order. Our environment, our systems of government—in fact everything seeks maximum entropy. Everything constantly moves towards a state of maximum disorder.

On the one hand, this is a depressing concept. One could become fatigued just imagining the ongoing effort that is necessary to prevent this degeneration of our personal lives and our societies. No matter what we do on Monday, come Tuesday the world will do its best to undo Monday's efforts of sorting, cleaning, and organizing. So our cars get dirty, or our desks get a bit more cluttered. These things are not a big deal. But keeping crime under control or keeping the electricity on and the water running—these things are a bit more urgent, and the same forces that mess up our closets are making every effort to insure that these endeavors also fail. This is one reason why freedom is so hard to maintain in our world. Freedom requires order, and as we have just seen, this is not so easy to sustain.

But there is another way to view this idea of entropy and disorder, a way that is far less discouraging. Since we are now well aware of all the infinite ways in which our world could have been constructed, entropy is another clue to the puzzle of why our world is this specific way. Our universe could disdain entropy. Instead of eggs cracking, never to be whole again, cracked eggs could fly off of the floor and reassemble themselves. Ridiculous? In our universe, yes, of course. But that's only because it's the only world we know. In this sense we are no different than that little girl we met in the previous chapter, the one who assumes that her family's patterns are universal. Dinner at six, butter on both sides of the bread, and milk for dinner—it's all she knows. Another universe (which may in fact exist) could be constructed in such a way that people in that universe would never imagine the possibility of a universe with a preference for chaos. Order would be the norm, disorder the exception. Equilibrium would be weird, disorder unheard of.

We reside in a universe that seeks maximum entropy. Since it is but one option out of an infinite set of possibilities, it is significant that it is so. We must expend energy to bring order to chaos, to bring light to darkness, to bring beauty to ugliness. We must do so continually, or chaos, darkness and ugliness will win every time. This is not news. A laissez-faire approach always results in disorder. Filth and anarchy have the advantage. Now you know why. Entropy.

Entropy may be powerful, but there is an even greater force. While filth and anarchy may have the advantage of being the default state, they only win if we let them. Humans have the power to overcome this immense force called entropy. If we choose to expend the energy, *we* will win every time. Want a clean park where your children can play? Put in the effort to pick up all the empty cans and broken bottles, plant grass and trees, and you will have your perfect park. No unseen force of nature will stop you. If you want democracy and freedom, you can have that as well. Educate your neighbors, work together to build a strong economy, hold each other responsible for actions, and democracy and freedom will follow. No invisible cosmic forces will prevent it from happening if you—and many, many others of like mind—wish it to be so.

Entropy can be defeated by mankind every single time if mankind is willing to expend the required energy. We can and will win anytime we so choose. It's as if your favorite sports team could decide that morning at breakfast, "Hey, how about we win today?" and know for sure that victory was guaranteed.

Humans are in this sense incredibly powerful. How often do we, individually, feel powerless to change not only our own reality but that of the world? Repairing the world seems beyond imagination. Poverty, injustice, and disease seem unbeatable. They of course have entropy on their side. But whatever or whoever is responsible for our particular universe—many would call it God—has endowed humanity with an even greater power, the power to defeat entropy every single time. Some would call that omnipotence, and in fact that is just what it is. Keep that in mind for later. For now, it is simply another clue: Something is going on here.

chapter eight

HISTORY

L eonardo da Vinci lived in the latter half of the fifteenth and
early part of the sixteenth centuries. He was an exceptional artist
as well as a scientist and inventor. What he was not was intellectually free. Leonardo, just like everyone else in Italy at this time,
relied on nobility and the Church for his support, for those two entities decided who did what where. Academic and intellectual freedom
were not the order of the day. While Leonardo created an incredible
body of work in both the arts and sciences, he was unquestionably
limited by the order of his world. Who knows what else he could have
accomplished if he had had the freedom to work as he pleased without regard for meeting the expectations and limits placed on him by
his benefactors?

Each of us is similarly limited by our circumstances. We have been
assigned coordinates of space and time, and we must function within
the parameters established by our particular space and time. We are
constrained today not so much by rules set by a church (unless you happen to be under the rule of an Islamic government) or a class of people, as was Leonardo, but more by the limits of our knowledge and
understanding. We know a great deal about science, yet there is much
that remains unknown. Physicists tell us that the majority of matter in
the universe is "dark matter," and that "dark energy" represents the bulk
of energy in the universe, and yet they have no idea what either of these
majorities actually represents. Without a firm understanding of these
entities, physicists possess an incomplete knowledge of the composition of the universe.

As I hope you have already seen, the same is true when we try to understand our role in this world. Our vision is markedly imperfect as we struggle to comprehend the nature of human life and our place in this particular universe. We often attempt to improve that understanding by analyzing history. "To ignore history is to repeat it," we have repeatedly heard. As we have discussed, we do in fact ignore history, not occasionally but on a daily basis. We repeat the same errors regularly, both as individuals and as societies, and as I have also pointed out, this fact is an important clue in our analysis. Since this is the case, it's a very small leap to pose the following question. Why bother with history?

Knowledge for its own sake is valuable. An educated populace is far more tolerant, far more open to investigation and introspection. Educated people live better and longer lives. Learning history—learning almost anything—broadens the mind and enriches life. History is both enlightening and entertaining. I encourage the study of history for those reasons.

What I don't encourage is the belief that the study of history is somehow going to save us from future disasters. Knowledge of historical events rarely prevents the repetition of actions and attitudes from days of old. What have we learned from the innumerable wars fought throughout recorded history? That war is most often a bad idea? So far that knowledge has not seemed to make a dent in our proclivity to wage it. How about the idea that all people, regardless of race, religion, or ethnicity, seek freedom—personal, intellectual, and political—and that eventually an oppressed people will rise up and demand such freedoms? No, that concept seemingly hasn't as yet taken hold either.

It's not that we don't "learn" from history. We do. We just choose to ignore what we have learned, because our personal narratives trump those lessons. History is rife with the story of fallen tyrants, yet there is no shortage of those who would strive to be the next all-powerful despot. Even if it won't last forever, the potential despot might figure that a good long run, or even a short one, as the man in charge is worth the effort. Power and wealth are irresistible for many, regardless of the likely ultimate outcome.

Our retelling of history is in itself instructive. Pick up any historical text and read the narrative of a particular event. Cause and effect are documented and dissected. A movement inexorably swells as the requisite elements become available. Soon a spark is ignited, triggering some explosion, and all hell breaks loose. In retrospect it is all so neat and clear, so why was it so difficult to identify while the contributing factors were coalescing? Why didn't anyone see it coming? We know hindsight is 20/20, but why is there so little foresight?

Most historical events feature central figures, a star or several stars. They are the leads in the play, and we carefully analyze their early years to uncover the impetus for their involvement in the event. "Ah, yes," we say, "it is clear why he chose this path. His mother had died and his father was loveless. So he relinquished his position and became an outsider, ready to foment his cause." As if it were a movie, and he were following a script.

Actually, that is precisely what history is: actors following scripts, and we are the actors. Although the play that is life has been repeatedly performed by the millions who came before, we are still obliged to read our lines. History does not relieve us of this responsibility to read our own lines and to act out our own personal parts. And while each of us is well aware of the ultimate outcome of our own personal play, death in no way minimizes the importance of acting out our own personal script. That is why history is not all that critical. Regardless of what has come before, regardless of history, each of us *must* execute our assigned part; this is what life is.

Studying history is important if we wish to broaden our vision and our intellect and to create educated and thoughtful citizens who can contribute to the world at a high level. Ignorance is a far greater disease than cancer or HIV/AIDS; ignorance has killed and will kill millions. Studying history, however, will not save the world from the next misadventure.

Of course the question is, once again, why? Why do we repeat the same errors that our ancestors committed, again and again and again? Why are we still waging war, why are we still oppressing others? Why must we act out our parts as if the play had never before been performed? Are we really so blind that we can't see that all of this, every nuance of life, has already been played out innumerable times in other productions by other actors? All we need do is review history. History reveals that tyrants are always overthrown, that all people seek freedom, and that if people are allowed to be free, they will prosper to a greater degree than would be so if some are oppressed. This doesn't seem all that difficult, so why do we insist on repeating every act of this play time and again? It is undeniable that this is how the world works, that despite our knowledge of history we repeat the same behaviors unendingly. By now it should be clear to you what the next line is: SOMETHING IS GOING ON HERE.

Arguments exist on the goal of Darwinian evolution. Is it the individual or the species, or something else that seeks to prevail? Over the past few decades the gene, the genetic information stored in our cells, has been promoted as the basic unit of natural selection. Whatever the basic unit of natural selection, competition among and within species requires that individuals who hope to survive must adapt to changing environments; the most successful in doing so are the winners, and they and their genes go on, forward into time. Those who cannot adapt and who cannot meet the challenges are destined to fail. Well over 90 percent of all species that ever existed on this planet have become extinct and have been replaced by—or have turned into—more successful species. This process continues invisibly and perpetually. We might assume that this is also true of humans, since we are but another species that shares the earth. Homo sapiens, as a species—as is true of every other species—seeks immortality, so we do what we need to do to guarantee our survival.

This last paragraph is what might be termed the "conventional wisdom." Suppose, however, that the basic assumption, that we are collectively driven by an invisible requirement to perpetuate something—species, individual, or gene—is incorrect. Suppose that we have misread the evidence and that mankind's purpose on Earth is not survival and the perpetuation of the any of these. Suppose, contrary to this scientific theory, that neither our genes nor our species are actually competing to carry on generation after generation. So far in this book we have seen that the world is often far different than we have imagined. Concepts that we have take for granted, those that we just assume represent the natural state of nature, may in fact not be correct. When you alter the basic assumptions of any experiment or investigation, everything that follows must be re-evaluated in a completely different light.

As history proceeds, we imagine a species that is moving to higher and higher levels of knowledge, achievement, and purpose. We look back on the Middle Ages and find it to be an era of ignorance and brutality. The people of today's developed nations seem far more evolved than their counterparts a thousand years in the past. If we stop for a moment and reflect on this, we might find that we are a bit less certain of our conclusion. How *has* the world changed over that expanse of time?

Our technology would be nothing less than witchcraft or magic to someone from the Middle Ages. We shop for food; we don't hunt for it. We live in climate-controlled lodgings; we need not freeze in the winter or broil in the summer. What seemed to be a great distance back then can now be covered in minutes or hours in cars or planes rather than on foot or horseback. Email and telephones allow instantaneous communication no matter our geographical location on the planet. Who could argue that anything today, other than human emotions, resembles anything from that era?

Did those people who lived during the Middle Ages question their reason for being? Of course they did. Here we are, a millennium down the road of history, and still we pose the same question. While our environment has been entirely transformed, while every facet of life has been altered during this interval, still we seek the answer to the same fundamental question, life's meaning. And still we have no explanations. Even though we have not yet solved the riddle of man's purpose on Earth, it is fair to assume that that purpose has not changed since the Middle Ages, whatever it is. Our lifestyles and our technologies are completely different today than they were a thousand years ago, and yet the same question of purpose remains.

This is a critical point. Since the twin questions of purpose and meaning remain the same today, phrased no differently than they were a thousand years in the past, technology, science, and the unraveling of many of the universe's secrets cannot be the critical elements in this quest. Why? Because these change over time, while our questions remain static. They are not one whiff different than they were a thousand or even five thousand years ago. While technology and science are fascinating and should be perpetually pursued, they cannot be essential components in the formulation of life's purpose. We must look elsewhere.

I need to be clear before we proceed. Knowledge, whether scientific or experiential, has great value. The preceding paragraph should not be construed to be an attack on science or as a directive to substitute philosophy or religion in its place. Quite the contrary: ignorance is the enemy, not knowledge. My point is only that when we seek the answers to the question of life's purpose and meaning, science and technology alone cannot possibly provide the solutions. They can and do point out—as we discovered when we discussed the hard clues— that the world is not what we assume it to be, and this implies that something strange is afoot. What that something is lies beyond the realm of science and technology.

Although the study of history cannot provide relief from our future trials and tribulations, it nevertheless serves to enlighten. Choose a despot or dictator, any one from any age. He rises from out of nowhere, a charismatic and often brilliant manipulator of men at a time in history when his particular people are either led by a weak figure, are leaderless, or are in the midst of a great calamity or period of hopelessness. Soon he conquers his own nation and eventually others. He may display kindness towards his people, at least enough to keep them from revolting. Eventually, however, the lack of freedom, or lack of success, creates a groundswell either from within or without. He is finally brought down, or he dies; either way the reign ultimately ends. Nothing lasts forever. In retrospect thousands, or in the most egregious scenarios millions, perished or were oppressed for no good reason. There is never a good reason.

Fast forward fifty or a hundred or a thousand years, and the same scenario repeats, although with different actors and in a different setting. We recognize this to be true, even today. Yet we do not blow the whistle and say to each other, "Wait a minute. This is no different than events that we have repeatedly witnessed throughout history. Why don't we just not do this again?" Some would argue that if everyone were optimally educated and enlightened, if a deep and full knowledge of history were widely possessed, indeed we would not do it again. But while the frequency of such historical upheavals might be diminished with an informed populace, they would not be eliminated. This is because our personal narratives, our personal goals and needs, supersede any sense of communal responsibility. While we may *collectively* admit that it is wrong to take what is not ours, to deny rights and oppress others, and to commit violence against our neighbors, many of us skirt these rules when our lives and the lives of our loved ones are in play. To believe that an awareness of history will ever lead to a cessation of these acts is a mistake. It will not. Knowledge is wonderful. Knowledge is desirable. But knowledge will never be enough. As long as we individually hold the standard assumptions about life to be true—which we will discuss just below—we will continue to abuse, oppress, and otherwise act unkindly when we deem it "necessary."

What are these standard assumptions? Most of us see the world as a pyramid. We begin somewhere near the bottom and attempt to scale the structure and reach the pinnacle. Of course, a pyramid is far wider at the bottom than at the top. Only a few will be able to occupy the peak; the rest will fail somewhere along the way. It's not merely material possessions that are invoked in this scenario. Imagine your "perfect" life. Perhaps to you it's a family, a wife or husband, a child or two, a pet, good neighbors, and good health. To another it may be great wealth or power, or both. Most of us have some idea of that perfect life.

What would we do, what *do* we do, to reach the top of our own personal pyramid? We cheat, we lie (a lot), we steal, we abuse, we oppress, we condemn, we bear false witness against our neighbors. You get the idea. When we then get together as groups—religious groups, ethnic groups, tribes, national groups—we wreak far greater havoc. We do these things so that our group has a better chance than some other group of reaching the pyramid's pinnacle, and then within those groups we compete individually to reach the top.

The problem with that vision of a perfect or even a very good life is not that it is unattainable. For some, it actually is attainable. We all know people who have had incredibly blessed lives and who have gotten pretty much everything they have wanted. In fact, the book *The Secret*, by Rhonda Byrne, preaches that if you can learn to think correctly, you can get precisely what you want. Maybe you can, maybe you can't; that's not the issue (there's always that problem of being careful what you wish for). *It's the entire concept of the perfect life that is the issue.* If you have an image of what life should be and if the life you end up living bears no resemblance to the life you imagined, odds are you won't be very happy.

If our assumptions are correct—that life is indeed pyramidal in structure and that coming out on top is the goal—then everything we do to reach that goal makes perfectly good sense, even those nasty things we listed above. We may wish that we could behave in better ways, but ideas and actions that promote our success strike us as logical—and they are to be expected. This is why history is of little consequence in determining future actions. It's not that we are uneducable. It's that we are clever enough to know that we had better constantly promote our own personal agendas if we have any hope of coming out on top. We can't worry about Alexander the Great or Caesar or Hitler or even our Uncle Joe who had it and lost it. Their personal histories matter little; we still need to focus on our own path and do what we can to scramble up that pyramid.

Recall those figures we just mentioned. Alexander the Great—conqueror of an enormous empire, a man regarded as one of the greatest military minds in history—died at age thirty-three, possibly poisoned by an enemy. While his legacy endured, his empire crumbled soon after his death. No doubt millions perished under his reign. Julius Caesar, another brilliant military mind, became emperor of the Roman Empire. Once again millions were subjugated or murdered as the empire was being assembled. While we still recall him today, in some cases fondly, it's because a brilliant non-military man, William Shakespeare, wrote a masterful play based on his life. Caesar, of course, was assassinated.

Adolf Hitler rose from obscurity and became supreme ruler of a defeated and despondent Germany that was desperate for resurrection. What transpired as he created the Third Reich is all too familiar: brutality beyond comprehension, the murder of millions, and eventually the near complete destruction of Germany. Hitler was dead when the war concluded.

Each of these men rose to power swiftly, influenced the lives of millions, and then fell hard and left this earth as rapidly as they had ascended. This cycle is no accident. It has been and is perpetually repeated. Despots aren't the only ones who walk this path. Today's front-page photos often feature men and women who held great power, financial or political, and who were brought down by some personal failing. CEOs whose companies went bankrupt, politicians caught with both hands in the cookie jar or committing some incredible indiscretion, athletes or famous actors with personal disasters: all of these people live the same story. The rich and powerful seem to fall from grace daily.

Then there is the flip side, the victory of the poor or weak. How often have we heard the stories of those who have risen from the ashes, those whose lives were devastated and near their end, those who found a way to not only survive but to reach incredible heights of success? These up-and-down cycles of life are everywhere, and the phenomenon points to another clue. If life were truly a pyramid, if the point of a life was to reach the top, then once on top no one would fall. Arriving at the pinnacle would mean victory, mission accomplished. Bells would ring, flags would fly, God would send an angel to pluck you from the peak and welcome you into the Kingdom of Heaven. There would be no such thing as a fall from grace. You earned it, you keep it, you win.

Of course that is not how our world works. We slip and slide through the course of our lives. Sometimes we're on top, other times we're brought low, but most of the time we are somewhere in transition. Once again we should appreciate that our world need not have been constructed in this manner. It could have been created so that once we have reached the top we are never displaced. Those at the bottom would have zero chance of improving their lives, no matter the circumstance. Our world could have been constructed in such a way, but it wasn't. It was constructed in a very specific manner: there are no guarantees of long-lasting power, but there are also no fixed positions at the bottom. Our actions and behaviors have the power to change our state of affairs.

It is this unlimited power, the power of the possible, that is so fascinating. Just as we can defeat entropy, our personal development is not constrained by the natural state of the world. Some would argue that this statement is simply untrue. Poverty, like ankle irons, keeps many at the bottom of the heap. Illness or congenital limitations similarly suppress others. The opportunity for some of life's luxuries, and certainly some necessities like food and shelter, is not fairly or universally distributed.

This apparent lack of fairness, however, does not equate with an inability to live a fulfilling and meaningful life. That can happen only when we assume that the goal of life is to make a successful ascent of the pyramid that we have described. If instead of a pyramid a different paradigm is in fact in play in our world, then those assumptions about life's possible limitations will be erroneous.

Each of us is required to play our parts and utter our lines, even though all possible parts have been performed many times before. This is not in doubt. "All the world's a stage, and all the men and women merely players," Shakespeare correctly teaches us in *As You Like It*. The show must go on for each of us as if we are the first, as if nothing ever preceded our appearance on the stage of life. This is why we don't remain at the zenith of our accomplishments and why we are never destined to remain at the bottom. This is why a knowledge of history cannot prevent future misadventures or calamities. The purpose of life, as we will see, is wrapped up in this requirement to play out our individual roles regardless of what has come before.

A Tale of Two Families

"Blessings are like blue-plate specials, Robert, good today only. Take advantage of them while they are here, and never take them for granted. Man plans and God laughs. Have you heard that before? It's one of my favorites. You don't think He is watching and paying attention? Let me tell you a little story."

Each time I heard that introduction I smiled like a child just informed of an imminent trip to the ice cream shop; something tasty was on its way.

"Sit down, Robert," he began. "It might take me a bit longer to relate this one to you. It's been a while since I've recounted this tale, so I hope you will grant an old man some leeway."

Are you kidding? I thought. First of all, this "old man" was sharp as a tack. I had never met anyone even half his age who could hope to keep up with that seasoned mind. And hurrying was the last thing I wished him to do. I could think of nothing more enjoyable than to sit and listen, for at the least I would be entertained by an expert storyteller. And I would be much more likely to finish this session with Dr. Benjamin a good deal wiser than I had begun.

"This is the tale of two boys, two lives which diverged from the moment of conception. Their names were Rudy and James. Do you think names are important, Robert?"

By the time I had heard a few of Dr. Benjamin's stories, I had begun to realize that they were not simple, passive lectures where the teacher spoke and the student merely listened. These were interactive experiences, and the student was expected to partici-pate——more often as foil than as a true participant, but that was part of his plan.

"No?" I guessed, as if I were back in my American short story class. I'd taken that class as an elective in my junior year of college, solely for the purpose of sitting next to Peggy Kearns, a girl on whom I had one hellacious crush. Since my entire *raison d'etre* for being in that class was to stare at her and fantasize of our would-be lives together, I paid little attention to the readings or the class discussion. Inevitably, Professor Sorrens would call my name when I was in the depths of a drooling trance. Upon recognizing the sound of my name, which usually was uttered at least twice as Professor Sorrens sought to rouse me from my emotional stupor, I would attempt to re-orient as quickly as possible, play back the tape of the last few moments of class discussion (which fortunately my subconscious had so generously recorded while I was off in fantasyland), process the limited information available, and take a wild stab at the answer. Even I was amazed how often I was actually in the ballpark, and Professor Sorrens, who appropriately questioned my devotion to the field of the American short story, was held at bay, not quite able to squash me this time around. Of course, he would have ample opportunities to do so later.

"Is that a guess, Robert?" Dr. Benjamin said. "You are entitled to an opinion. What do you think? Are names important? There is not necessarily a right or wrong answer."

"No, I don't think they are, sir. A rose by any other name and all of that."

"Interesting, Robert, but I am afraid incorrect. Of course names are important. They are not the only thing that is important, or the most important, but they are significant. What we call something matters; language is not irrelevant. Sounds are important, Robert. They convey essence, texture, relationships. And names are sounds. We do not name things or people randomly, do we? We choose names carefully, because they conjure thoughts and visions. Names are important, Robert. You may want to keep that in mind."

With that lesson delivered, Dr. Benjamin began the tale he had promised.

■ ■ ■

James was born into affluence. His father had invested in land long before any of his contemporaries could envision their town's inevitable growth as the automobile industry took hold and flourished. James's father had that vision and more, for as he sold off property to build the houses, the retail establishments, and the factories that were required in increasing numbers, he also had the vision to invest in some of those enterprises. Over the course of several years, he accumulated enough real estate and other investments to guarantee the financial security of several generations.

Since money would never be an issue, James enjoyed no shortage of academic and non-academic opportunities. As if this were not enough, James was also blessed with considerable athletic skills, and that natural ability, coupled with many hours of private lessons in various sports, created a remarkable athlete, and eventually a local phenomenon. Football hero, basketball standout, and star pitcher for the high school baseball team—this was James's life.

For every James there are a thousand Rudys. Rudy's father had died in a factory accident when Rudy was still a child. Rudy's father was a welder, and there had been discussion among the welders in the factory for several months about the risk of keeping flammable gasses in the work area of the factory. The storage areas which had been designated for the gas tanks had been taken over to make room for an expansion of operations, and the gas tanks had been relocated to the factory floor. As work progressed, the tanks were repeatedly moved until eventually they ended up perilously close to the welders' station. The tragedy feared by the welders one day occurred—an errant spark ignited a massive explosion. At the age of twelve Rudy found himself fatherless.

Rudy's father's income was modest and had been enough to pay the family bills, but it left little for savings. Rudy's dad had planned to buy some life insurance when he got his next raise and could get his head above water, but that day never came. Rudy's mother was left with a mortgage, three children, and no income other than some meager death benefits from the factory.

Rudy and James were the same age and attended the same school. Occasionally they shared a teacher, but that was the extent of their contact. Rudy knew James; everyone knew James. He was the kid with the dream life—rich, the most popular, a super athlete—the life to which everyone at school aspired, and on more than one occasion Rudy would close his eyes and imagine it.

If only I could be James.

James did not know Rudy. It was not that James was a snob or that he felt above those of Rudy's socioeconomic class. On the contrary, James had been raised well and had been taught from an early age that his good fortune made him no better than anyone else.

Since Rudy had had to work after school to help support his family, he could not engage in extracurricular activities, including sports, as James could. Even if Rudy had had the time for these things, it is unlikely that the paths of the two boys would have crossed. At least not very often.

Toward the end of high school, the world abruptly changed for each of these boys. It seems that James's father had had a bit of help in acquiring his land. The vision was indeed his, but the money required to purchase the land was not readily accessible to him, so he had struck a deal to secure a loan from some less-than-scrupulous individuals. James's father knew these men and was aware that their methods of acquiring capital were not always above the law, but he was anxious to fulfill his dreams and so took their money in exchange for part ownership in his properties and other investments. James's father's partners were involved in acquiring black-market items through nefarious means, and as payback for their "generosity," they frequently required James's father to help them move or store this merchandise until a buyer became available. The law caught up with his partners, and after a detailed investigation they were arrested and convicted. As part of their sentence they were required to pay taxes on their illegal gains, as well as a monumental fine. Since they owned a significant part of James's father's assets, the holdings were liquidated to fulfill the obligation. Although James's father was not charged with any crime in return for his testimony, he lost nearly everything he had accumulated.

As James and his family slid down the curve of prosperity, Rudy's family soared. You remember, Robert, that I told you that Rudy had worked after school to help support his family. Rudy's first job was with an accountant. The accountant had a new client, a young man who was attempting to manufacture electronics that could be used to regulate the mixture of air and gas in automobiles. The founder of this small automobile parts company had called the accountant late one afternoon to finalize the financial documents which were necessary to complete a loan from the bank that next day, without which the young entrepreneur would not be able to acquire the necessary supplies to meet his contractual obligations. If he could not deliver the prototype by week's end, his customer, a large automotive conglomerate, would cancel the contract and in effect close this small business. Time was of the essence. Trouble was, the accountant—not knowing the urgency of this situation— had left the office early that day, and he was nowhere to be found. Our young businessman was near hysteria until Rudy recalled that the accountant had mentioned a drive out of town, about an hour away, to visit a breeder in order to choose a new dog for his children. Since it was to be a surprise for his kids, he had kept his trip a secret. Rudy was the only one who knew.

Rudy heard the stress in the young owner's voice as he conveyed the urgency of the situation. Rudy promised him nothing less than his best effort. He borrowed his mother's car, and with only a vague idea of the location of this breeder, he set out to find his boss. Of course he succeeded—it wouldn't be much of a story now, would it Robert, if he hadn't—and the loan was secured. Our young entrepreneur was so grateful that he immediately hired Rudy to be his part-time assistant. He could only pay Rudy a very small salary, because money was tight. Instead, he offered Rudy stock in his fledgling company. Within two years, he had perfected the electronics, and sales went through the roof. The company's success was soon common knowledge, and before long the owner was fielding offers from large corporations interested in acquiring his business. He held out for a while, and when he thought his company had reached its maximum value he sold the company to his largest customer at a price that exceeded his best hopes. All of that stock that Rudy had been given in lieu of pay was suddenly worth a great deal. For Rudy and his family, that stock meant a new home, college for Rudy and his siblings, and enough so that his mother would never have to worry about money for as long as she lived.

But this isn't a story about serendipity and how fortunes can rise and fall like the tides. The story of Rudy and James does not end with the sudden reversal of fortunes that each experienced. Both went to college, and both graduated full of hopes and dreams, their pasts neatly stowed so as not to diminish their futures. Life for each of them was a clean slate; the days ahead were pristine sheets of white paper with not a word yet inscribed.

Through his relationship with the owner of the electronics firm, Rudy was able to secure a management training position with a large automotive company. Rudy was a determined student, and he was eager to replicate the success of his mentor and one day build his own company. After two years of training, Rudy graduated to his first management position—working in supply procurement for the company. After another two years, he felt he had learned enough and resigned from the company to start his own distribution firm. He was looking for eager young men and women to join him, so he began searching the surrounding counties for likely prospects. James had been working as an assistant to the procurement manager at a small firm, and through word of mouth he learned of Rudy's new company. He called Rudy, sent him his resume, and within a week had received a message on his answering machine to come for an interview.

Remember, Rudy knew of James from high school. Here was a great irony, he thought to himself. The great James—school hero, rich kid—now asking him, Rudy, for a job. Rudy could not ignore this opportunity to strut. James had gotten it all without a stitch of effort, while he, Rudy, had lost his father at so young an age and had to work hours upon hours to help support his mother and siblings. Yes, he would hire James, if for no other reason than to see how James would fare without his father and his money to grease his path.

James joined Rudy's company, and though he did so begrudgingly, Rudy acknowledged that James was talented and hard-working. He had misjudged him, he thought, and began to consider bringing James onto the executive team of his rapidly growing company. About six months after James had joined Rudy's company, a representative from a regional automotive parts company came by to talk with Rudy. He took a tour of the facility prior to his meeting with Rudy and while on his tour spotted James, whom he recognized from his high school athletic days as that excellent pitcher for the opposing school's baseball team. As it happened, this representative's father had worked for James's father in one of his factories, so although he had never met James, he knew of him.

The representative ended his tour at Rudy's office. "Hi," he said, extending his hand. "I'm Joseph Scullen from Great Plains Automotive."

"I'm Rudy Thomlinson. Thanks for coming."

They spoke about business for awhile, and then Joseph Scullen, in an attempt to move the relationship forward, noted that he had seen an old high school competitor during his tour of the facility.

"Oh yes, James Ronston. We went to the same high school." Rudy was careful not to mention that they went to high school together; that was surely not the case in his mind.

Joseph told Rudy that it was quite a coincidence that his own father had worked for James's father in his factory. "My dad," Joseph said, "told me about how James's father's company had been involved in a financial scandal, and how he had lost the business. It cost my dad his job when the company went under. Seems as though the company was also acting as a storage warehouse for stolen goods. My dad remembered how they used to surreptitiously move equipment and supplies from one site to another, and no one knew why at the time, but it was all to hide the stolen merchandise. Sad part is that my dad told me they moved some dangerous materials one time to a place where sparks were flying and it caused an explosion where a worker was killed. I remember my dad telling me that at least he had lost only a job, not his life."

Rudy froze. The color drained from his face. A wave of nausea enveloped him and he felt as if he would lose consciousness.

"Are you all right?" Joseph asked. Rudy began to tremble. Joseph grabbed a chair and positioned it to catch the slumping Rudy. After a minute, Rudy began to regain his composure.

"My father," he muttered.

"What?" Joseph could barely hear the whisper.

"That was my father," Rudy repeated. "The man who was killed was my father."

Joseph was stunned. He felt like a little boy in a lingerie shop who, although he was young, knew enough to know that that he did not belong in that situation and desperately wanted out.

"I am so sorry." There was nothing else to say. Fortunately for Joseph, Rudy regained his composure.

"Thank you for coming, Joseph. I'll be in touch with you about our order."

And with that, Rudy led Joseph to the door.

■ ■ ■

When he was alone again, shock became rage. *My father was killed because James's dad was a criminal, a man who cared more, much more, about money than he did about people.*

Rudy picked up the phone. "Don, it's Rudy," he said to his procurement manager. "You are to fire James immediately."

Rudy told Don to calculate how much money James was due for this current pay period, to double it as a severance package, to have Joanne issue him a check for that amount, to hand it to James as he fired him, and to collect his keys and parking card before he left the building.

James had absolutely no idea why he was fired so abruptly, and despite many attempts to contact Rudy, he was not able to speak with him. All he knew was what Don, his manager, had told him— which wasn't much. Rudy always had his reasons, Don had said. Take the money and move on to something new. In time, James did just that. He started his own business and found a wonderful woman with whom he shared three healthy children.

One day his oldest son, James Jr., who had inherited his father's athletic prowess and was training as a young Olympian, was delivering the town's advertising newspaper to the local neighborhoods. He loaded up his two shoulder sacks and walked house to house, depositing the tabloid in each mailbox.

As he was closing one of the boxes, he heard a car come screeching around the corner, filled with teenagers who apparently were celebrating that afternoon's victory of their school's football team. The driver was clearly distracted by all the activity within the car and did not notice the red kickball rolling out into the street in front of him, or the six-year-old boy hot in pursuit. But James Jr. did. He dropped his sacks, tore after the child, lifted the young boy, and literally threw him out of the way of the oncoming vehicle. The boy was safe, but the fender of the car caught James Jr.'s left leg, snapping it almost in half. James's son recovered enough after three surgeries to walk, but his plans to one day compete as an Olympic decathlete were, like his leg, shattered.

Naturally the press heard of the incident and of James Jr.'s exploits. It was big news, as was the carelessness of the teenagers who had injured James's son and almost took the life of the small boy. James was deeply saddened by his son's lost dreams, but he was so proud of him for saving the little boy. He read of the reckless teenagers who had cost James Jr. his dreams and who had almost taken the life of that boy. The driver of the car was one Dennis Thomlinson. James did not notice that the surname of the teenage driver was the same as that of his former boss, Rudy Thomlinson.

But Rudy Thomlinson also watched the news with particular interest, because his son had been driving that car. It had been his son who had almost killed a young child, his son who had cost that brave young man his athletic aspirations. And he recognized the name of that brave young man, James Ronston, and once again the same wave of nausea he had experienced the day he learned of the cause of his father's death swept over him.

"My God,' he cried. "My God!"

Rudy called James. "We need to talk, James. *I* need to talk. Will you meet me tomorrow?" James agreed, and the next morning the two of them sat together on a bench in the park.

Rudy recounted the events they had in some way shared over the years, especially the most recent that had brought the lives of their sons together. Rudy broke down and sobbed, and he asked James to forgive him. Repeatedly, he thanked James for his son's heroics—for surely they had saved his own son's life as well. Because of James Jr., a small boy had not died at the hand of Dennis, Rudy's son.

James looked at Rudy, placed his arm around Rudy's shoulder, and in a voice full of grace, he began to speak.

"It kind of makes you want to smile, doesn't it Rudy? For some reason we are somehow attached, you and me. Our families. Our fates are linked, perhaps for generations to come. Each step one of us takes in some way influences the life of the other. I don't understand why, Rudy, and probably I will never know why. But it seems to me that's just the way it is. My dad taught me something long ago, something I have shared with my children. And I want to share it with you. Life is like a nine-inning baseball game, Dad would say. You have to play until the final out. Never get complacent or too full of yourself, because just when you think you have the game in hand, the scores can really change."

And through the torrent of tears and chest-heaving sobs, Rudy did smile. He smiled because the struggles of his childhood, the death of his father, and all that he had witnessed to this point in his life suddenly had meaning.

■ ■ ■

Dr. Benjamin paused. He seemed to look right through me to a scene only he could view. Then, as if suddenly returning from a reverie, he straightened himself, displayed that warm smile that has won over every patient he has ever treated, and said, "The scores really *can* change, Robert, and they often do. Man plans, God laughs. And now story time is over. Time to get back to work."

chapter nine

MAN PLANS
GOD LAUGHS

L et me share with you my own personal life plan, which I concocted when I was nineteen years old. At that time, I was in my third year at a small liberal arts college in the state of New York. My parents were alive and well and were living in a suburb of New York City. We lived in a modest house in a very nice middle-class neighborhood. My father owned a small business with his brother in the garment district of New York City. His business struggled, but he managed to keep his head just above water. My mother worked as a saleswoman in a women's boutique clothing store. She had at one time owned her own store but was now working for someone else. I had one sister who had recently married and was living in Canada.

College was going very well. As a biology major, pre-med, my grades were very good. I had many friends, a girlfriend, and fun was not in short supply. My greatest concerns were the next physics exam and what to do the following weekend. It seemed like a good time to solidify my personal life agenda. I would of course finish college and go directly to medical school. How to fund medical school never crossed my mind; my dad would figure that out. After medical school I would probably get married, have a couple of kids, and enjoy my profession. Basically the plan was to live happily ever after.

Here is what actually transpired over the ensuing couple of years. Just after my twentieth birthday I learned that my father had developed cancer of the head and neck, likely from his lifelong love affair with cigars. Within eighteen months, he was gone. I mentioned earlier that my father's business was precarious. Turns out it was more precarious than I had imagined. Not only was he gone, but so was the money. Six weeks after my father's funeral, my mother sold our home to generate some cash and promptly moved to Florida. Although I had scored quite high in the medical school admissions test, I did not gain acceptance to any medical school on my first attempt. Despite my good grades and test scores, my Vietnam protesting activity did not sit well with the chairman of the pre-med committee at my college, and my lukewarm recommendations reflected his disdain for my political activities.

So less than two years after the formulation of my happily-ever-after plan, I was without a father—and effectively a mother—a home, a career, or much of anything, including money. I was twenty-one years old, and my youth had come to an abrupt and jarring end. At the time I was not sufficiently astute to recognize that the strange sound I was hearing was God's laughter.

Dumb luck, divine intervention—who knows what other forces of nature were at play. But about a year later I did gain acceptance to medical school, and miraculously I was granted a full scholarship. Two years hence I married my girlfriend, and after another two years completed medical school and moved to Washington, D.C. for my internship and residency. Three beautiful children followed, and once again life was near perfect. I was back on track to "happily ever after."

Or so I thought. My marriage grew increasingly difficult as the years passed. Finally it reached the breaking point after seventeen years. Divorced, part-time single parent of three children—who would have guessed this was in my future? Certainly not I. If someone had asked me five years earlier if I would ever get divorced, I would have convincingly established that this was an impossible outcome, at least in my life and in my future. The laughter was louder this time, but this time I knew what it was. God was at it again.

Of course, my personal story has continued. It ebbs and flows. And so does yours—and everyone else's in this world. My narrative is hardly unique, and the adversity I was confronted with pales in comparison to the adversity faced by less fortunate people around the globe. Life rarely goes as planned, and my story is simply one out of billions that reflects that truth.

What are we to make of this phenomenon, if anything? Is it "just the way it is" and that's the end of it? As Sigmund Freud once said, "Sometimes the cigar in my mouth is just a cigar." But it's hard to ignore the notion that the final product of life—the completed personal narrative—may in fact hinge on the unexpected consequences of our changing fortunes. Put more simply, curveballs are the rule, not the exception. Let's return to my personal account to illustrate.

I have often described my twenty-second year of life—the turbulent year when I lost my father and then dealt with all of the repercussions that followed that event—as an experience similar to being pushed from a high cliff into freezing water without a life vest. I didn't drown, and although I was stunned for a good long while, I managed to not only survive but in many ways thrive. Had I not been rather dramatically dissociated from my support system, I doubt I would have become as independent and self-sufficient. My sense of personal responsibility and my commitment to assisting others would likely have been far weaker. Of course I cannot claim that any one event guaranteed another, but it is fair to say that the events of that time in my life dramatically shaped the years that followed.

In turn I have had an impact on the lives of many others. They in turn will influence the lives of still others, and so on and so on. It is said that there are no ordinary moments or ordinary events, and this is true. As we live our lives, we learn and evolve, and we pass that knowledge on to others who in turn do the same. It is one enormous cascade.

Recall the story of the father and his friend, the firefighter, from chapter eight. The most minute actions can have unimaginable effects. We continually make plans; most are barely worth noting. "After work I'll stop at the bank and then the dry cleaner. I'll take my child to soccer practice, then pick up something for dinner." Some are a bit more long range. "We just bought plane tickets to California for our vacation this summer. I know it's only January, but the fares were great. We'll plan the rest later on." And then there are those plans we make for the more distant future: marriage, career, and retirement.

Meteorologists are often chastised for their inability to accurately predict the weather more than a day in advance. Most Internet weather sites have a tab for the ten-day forecast. Write it down for your town today, and check the accuracy ten days from now. Chances are some days will be right on, others ridiculously off base. That's the nature of weather. Since there are so many variables, it is impossible to predict the weather with perfect accuracy in advance. I am amused by the climatologists' predictions about the world's temperatures decades from now. While I am all for conservation and decreasing our use of fossil fuels, it's not because I place any faith in their predictions. If they can't be certain of the weather this weekend, how am I to believe they have any ability to anticipate the climate fifty years hence?

In his book, *The Black Swan*, Nassim Nicholas Taleb makes an excellent case that we cannot reliably predict future events. What's more, the events that most influence our world are in fact those that are the most unpredictable. He calls such occurrences *black swan events*. September 11, 2001 and the rapid progression of the Internet are two such black swan events; history is full of many more. Just as we cannot predict the far future's weather, we likewise have no chance of predicting significant future occurrences.

So what does this mean? It means that the world simply unfolds; there is nothing we can do to significantly alter events or stop the process. Considering the power we believe we have as humans—the power to create (and destroy), the power to literally change the course of rivers and move mountains, the power to harness nature's resources to fit our desires—it is difficult to accept that we are in fact mostly powerless to predict and control future events. SOMETHING IS GOING ON HERE.

Here we have a most important clue. Despite all of our progress over the millennia, we are no more able to predict or control the future than we were thousands of years in the past. Of course we can control our immediate environments to some degree—we can be warm in winter and cool in summer, for example—but the more significant issues are beyond us. We cannot calm the winds of a hurricane or stop the earth from quaking.

What makes this a clue? We return to the concept presented several times earlier in this book: the world does not have to be this way. The universe could be predictable. Hurricanes and earthquakes could be calmed. We could control nature. We just assume that we can't and never will. But it could be so. The universe could have been constructed differently. Ours just wasn't.

Our lives are less like the pages of a book, neatly sequenced, and more like fresh popcorn pouring forth from the carnival's multi-colored machine once the heat is turned up. From the ordinary all-the-same kernels comes the excitement of exploded puffs of corn, each one unique and unpredictable. We have absolutely no idea what the next kernel will look like. We can't anticipate when the last kernel will pop, or which will be a dud. We similarly have no idea what will transpire from minute to minute in our own lives and in the lives of others. This is exciting but also quite frightening. The fickleness of life is paralyzing for some. Our husbands or wives, our children, our health, our safety and security, our livelihoods—all of it can vanish in an instant, or can just as easily persist for decades. We just don't know, and can't know. That is how our particular universe happens to work.

One could easily make the case that life is ridiculous. Albert Camus, the famous author and existentialist, did just that. More specifically, he referred to life as "absurd." Much of our time on Earth is a struggle. We work for those moments of happiness; we strive to transcend the mundane. But those beautiful moments are few and far between. We spend most of our time working to prevent the encroachment of entropy, just to keep ourselves going. For many, this alone embodies a sense of absurdity. For no matter how hard we work or how wonderful we are as human beings, we still will die, and this fact is—for Camus and people of like mind—ultimately absurd. We also know that no matter how well we plan or how careful we are, anything can happen—and we cannot predict how or when or if it will happen. We eat well and take vitamins, we exercise and rest, and then we suddenly die at age forty. We smoke and drink in excess, we live life at the edge, taking every risk imaginable, and then we die quietly in our sleep at age ninety-two. Many argue that this is proof that there is no master plan, no divine intervention, that life is completely random as well as absurd.

Actually the converse is more likely true. Recall again that the universe could be completely ordered, that entropy—that physical law that requires increasing disorder—could be inverted, that cracked eggs could become whole and that water could flow uphill. Another universe could exist where this is true. That good people die young, that the unhealthy can live a long, long time, that anything can happen to anyone—these are all facts about our particular universe. It's not "just the way it is." It's the way it is in *our particular universe*. Our universe could have been constructed so that these things would never happen. We assume that the "default" state of a world must involve randomness, and that randomness should characterize life. But in fact such an assumption ignores the reality that there is no one correct default state.

Life's serendipity makes for incredible experiences and constant learning. We wax poetic about this peculiarity of our universe, and there is a great deal to recommend it. Of course it's not so poetic for a young child when he or she loses a parent, or for a parent when she loses a child. It's not so poetic when a wall of water or a tornado wipes buildings and families from the earth. Those with chronic pain or illness and those for whom the simplest tasks are Sisyphean in nature may not be so impressed with the unexpected ups and downs that are the rhythm of life. But in the absence of turmoil and grief, perhaps most can agree that the serendipity of life *is* magnificent. What we often don't realize is that even at those times of tremendous stress and grief, the universe maintains its unpredictable beauty. At the moment of loss, precious little seems beautiful, but moments of beauty inevitably evolve from such moments. Incredible acts of kindness and generosity often flourish during those times. These unexpected events create huge shifts in direction for those involved. Their futures, and the futures of countless others, are dramatically altered and are often accompanied by unexpected benefits for the individual and his family, his friends, his community, and the entire world. It is not rare for great loss to be followed in due time by great accomplishment or great love.

Life unfolds. Our particular universe unfolds. It will do so until it ends—and end it will, just as each of our lives will end. Which brings us to death. The term seems so final, like the period at the end of this sentence. Man has struggled with this concept since the beginning of our time on Earth. Death begets so many questions. What happens when we die? Is this life all there is? If not, what comes next? We always assume that if there is a hereafter it will be better than our earthbound life. Freedom from our bodies—bodies which may have severely limited us at the end of our lives—freedom from hunger and sadness, freedom from all of the burdens of earthly life: this is what we expect in any respectable hereafter. Of course it may be that our life on Earth is the high point, that the hereafter is more difficult. Here is another question to which we have no certain answer.

One reason I believe we have had so much difficulty understanding death is that we have perpetually misunderstood life. Death has no meaning in the absence of life's meaning. Suppose I told you that the purpose of life is to grow old. If you grow old you are successful, and if not, you have failed. It matters not what kind of person you were or what you have accomplished in your life. The only noteworthy attribute you possess is your longevity. In that case, you would likely do whatever it takes to survive, no matter who or what obstructed your path to this goal.

If the purpose of life were to grow old, death would have a distinct significance. If you died at age ninety, you would see death as the awards ceremony at the end of your long contest. Not only would you not fear death, you would embrace it, since you had successfully completed your task and knew victory was yours. Should death arrive at age thirty, you would be devastated, since that would be a losing hand. You had not met the goal, for whatever reason, and it would not matter what that reason was. You would have failed. Frustration, sorrow, and maybe even fear would envelop you at the moment of your premature demise.

Instead of longevity, suppose that the purpose of life was to accumulate power and wealth. Again you might do whatever it took to achieve your goal, including trampling upon less savvy people who stand in your way. Ninety or thirty—death at either age would be unsettling and unsatisfactory. There would always be more wealth to acquire, more power to attain. At the moment of death, you likely would think, "If I only had another day, I could have gotten more."

Now consider death in the context of a life whose value is dependent on service to others. If you were consistently giving of yourself throughout your life whenever possible, you might still say at the moment of death, "If I only had another day, I could have done more, I could have helped another." I am reminded of Albert Schindler, the righteous German who saved hundreds of Jewish lives during the Holocaust and the protagonist of Steven Spielberg's movie *Schindler's List*. At the end of the movie, after the Germans were defeated and the concentration camp prisoners liberated, Schindler shed tears. If he had only tried harder, he felt, he could have saved more Jews from death. In this scenario—if service and kindness to others are your personal policy all the days of your life—then despite your disappointment at having to leave this world behind, you would be comforted by the knowledge that you had succeeded in your mission.

Our attitude at death is completely dependent on our approach to life. Death by itself has absolutely no meaning; death is in fact a relative concept. One cannot know if he or she should fear or welcome death without having some basis on which to make this determination. If you have met the requirements of life as you understand them and if you believe death to be the entrée into the next level, like mastering a video game, then you would welcome death at the completion of your mission. If you believe that there is no purpose to life and that death is absolutely final—ashes to ashes, dust to dust, and no great beyond—you would cling with all of your might to your last breath.

We must understand life to comprehend death. If I were asked to sum up the dominant attribute of life in a single word, that word would be "fragile." Imagine the most ornate crystal bowl, magnificent beyond description. As fabulous as it may be, it is always just a minor slip away from shattering. One might think of this as tragic, and in fact it is since the shattered pieces of glass have no value. Life is similarly magnificent, and also but a minor slip away from shattering.

One morning I was driving to work and listening to the news. A forty-two-year-old father of two, an attorney, had also been driving to work earlier that morning, probably also listening to his radio. A lumber truck was crossing an overpass just as this man was driving beneath the overpass. The driver of the lumber truck lost control of his vehicle, and the truck overturned. His load of lumber toppled over the edge of the overpass and landed on the roof of the car of the forty-two-year-old father of two traveling below. He was instantly killed. Just like that, forty-two years of effort were gone. Just like that, two young children were fatherless. Just like that, the worlds of many people were turned upside down.

We accept such events as just a part of life. We are sad but not surprised. We have heard this story or some minor variation of it hundreds if not thousands of times before. And despite this tragic event, life goes on for everyone. Life is different from there on out, but nonetheless it goes on. Isn't this odd? A tragedy occurs, and the world goes on. When any one of us experiences such a tragedy, we expect the world to stop and say, "We are so sorry. We won't work or play today. All trains and planes will immediately cease motion, and nothing at all will transpire until you tell us it is alright to proceed." Of course, little ceases at these times. Our own lives are incredibly disrupted, yet the rest of the world barely takes notice.

Even for the rich and famous, the most that can be expected is a more lengthy recognition of the life lost. While I was writing this book, Tim Russert, the respected NBC television journalist, suddenly and unexpectedly died. Over the ensuing weekend, the television news shows and even the print media were almost completely devoted to reviewing Mr. Russert's life and his accomplishments and to mourning his passing. Then came Monday, and Mr. Russert's death was no longer news. Little stops for long. We all keep going.

How is this even conceivable? We may have lost everything, may have suffered an indescribable tragedy. Yet the sun sets that evening and rises the next morning. Should a head of state or other famous person pass on, the sun will be undaunted. It's not only the sun that is unimpressed. Every animal and plant proceeds as if nothing has occurred, and in fact

well over 99.9% of all humans will do the same. This is nothing short
of remarkable: the universe and just about everything in it couldn't care
less if you die.

One reasonable deduction from this clear fact is that death—yours,
mine, an old woman's, a rich man's, a famous actor's or a homeless
person's—just can't be that big of a deal. It's a big deal to a barely measurable proportion of the earth's population, but to the rest of the universe it could not be less relevant. Extrapolating from that
assumption—the idea that any one death is irrelevant—it is quite
appropriate to deduce that any one *life* is irrelevant. That would be a
correct analysis only if the purpose of life was to influence or impress
the universe and its residents. If the purpose of each of our lives is to
influence the universe, then there is little reason to raise a child: he or
she will not succeed in significantly influencing the universe. Those who
think that life is a random biochemistry experiment would have every
reason to remain cynical.

We are presented with a conundrum. Death, and therefore any individual life, are seemingly irrelevant to the universe, yet we know instinctively that there is something precious about each life. How do we
reconcile these opposing concepts?

The solution to this problem is found outside of and separate from
the universe. While we live in the universe, it is not the universe to
which we are beholden. Life's purpose is not to influence or impress the
universe or anything within it; this much is already clear, since both of
these are impossible goals. While that conclusion does not bring us
much closer to identifying life's purpose, it does eliminate some broad
categories as possibilities. For example, fame cannot possibly be the target. Fame is derived from position or status, and as we have already
seen, no matter how famous one becomes the percentage of living creatures on the earth who are even remotely interested in your position or
status—even limiting the question to only humans—is miniscule. We
will spend a great deal of time in the final section of this book discussing the deductions we can draw from the clues we have assembled.
Death will serve as one of the most important clues to understanding
the purpose of life.

I have long been infused with the sense that God would not waste something as precious as a life. All of this energy that surrounds us, this "life energy," represents an enormous investment. Imagine each person as a toy powered by a battery. The sheer number of required batteries to power humanity is unimaginable, yet we just assume that they are readily available and disposable. A life is created, it is lived, it ends, and the battery by which it was powered disappears as mysteriously as it arrived. As a physician I understand the biochemistry of life, the role of oxygen and of the compound ADP in powering our cells. While the cycles that utilize sugars and fats are quite real and do provide the daily energy required to power our bodies, we are all aware that there is something more to the energy of life that defies clear explanation.

At the moment of death, something very specific happens. It's not just that cells stop functioning; something palpable occurs to that organism. The power is turned off, or more accurately the power is removed. If you have witnessed another's death, or even the death of a pet, you know what I mean. Even the physical appearance of the deceased changes instantaneously, as if a core component has been suddenly snatched away. Anyone witnessing this transformation instantly senses that something other than the cessation of a biochemical reaction has occurred.

Dr. Elisabeth Kubler-Ross was probably the most famous individual to deal with the issues of death and dying in the twentieth century. Thousands of medical and nursing students learned about death and dying from the writings of Dr. Kubler-Ross. While she was primarily noted for her identification and discussion of the five stages of grief, during her later years she focused on what happens at the moment of death. Her speeches and writings at this stage of her career are the most germane to our discussion in this book.

Dr. Kubler-Ross and her associates interviewed over twenty thousand individuals who had near-death experiences and spoke with countless numbers of dying patients. She described the sequence of events at death and spoke about deaths that she had witnessed. The transformations that this scientist and self-proclaimed skeptic witnessed forced her to see life and death in a completely different light.

Life and death and the world in which we live, she became convinced, were in fact not as they appeared to be. Sound familiar?

Were she alive today, she would tell you that she does not *think* but rather *knows* what occurs at death. Her speeches and writings attest to her certainty. I have chosen a few quotes from Elisabeth Kubler-Ross's writings and lectures which are nothing short of remarkable:

> When you leave the physical body, you are in an existence where there is no time. That simply means that time doesn't exist anymore. In the same way, one can no longer speak of space and distance in the usual sense because those are earthly phenomena.
>
> There are people awaiting you who died before you, who loved and treasured you a lot. And since time doesn't exist on this level, someone who lost a child when he was twenty years of age could, after his passing at the age of ninety-nine, still meet his child as a child. For those on the other side, one minute could be equal to one hundred years of our earth time.

When I read these words, a chill went up my spine. I had already learned, as you have in chapter four, that time as we understand it does not really exist. Past, present, and future, as Einstein told us, are just an illusion. Time does not flow: it just is. And here was a noted expert on death confirming in a metaphysical manner what I had already learned from hard physics.

One minute could be equal to one hundred years. Recall that light travels at the speed of light, and therefore all of its motion is through space; time stands still for light. If you were traveling on a light beam you would not age; time would be frozen. When Dr. Kubler-Ross discusses the relative nature of time and space from the perspective of death, she assures us that time does not flow after death. Time is revealed as the loaf of bread or the block of ice that we discussed in chapter four. All moments of time exist and therefore can be visited, theoretically. While we on Earth have no idea how to do this, Dr. Kubler-Ross describes this as not only possible but as a part of the reality of death. She describes time and space as "earthly phenomena" that are no longer relevant after death:

I'm going to share with you how you too can be convinced that this life, this time you are in a physical body, is a very, very short span of your total existence. It's a very important time because you are here for a very special purpose which is yours and yours alone. If you live well you will never have to worry about dying. You can do that even if you have only one day to live. The question of time is not terribly important; it is a man-made, artificial concept anyway.

Einstein and the physicists who followed him were interested in explaining observable phenomena. In fact, many physicists would tell you that they are not interested in what happens outside the observable universe since this cannot be measured. When I read Einstein, what struck me was just the opposite: what does his theory of special relativity tell us about the non-visible universe? Dr. Kubler-Ross in essence confirms Einstein's theory of special relativity, but in the context of the difference between life and death. Time is an earthly phenomenon, she insists, and is in fact an earthly illusion. Though they arrive at this conclusion from divergent approaches, Albert Einstein and Elisabeth Kubler-Ross would completely agree on this statement. She says:

> But my real job is, and this is why I need your help, to tell people that death does not exist. It is very important that mankind knows this, for we are at the beginning of a very difficult time. Not only for this country, but for the whole planet earth. Because of our own destructiveness. Because of nuclear weapons. Because of our greediness and materialism. Because we are piggish in terms of ecology, because we have destroyed so many, many natural resources, and because we have lost all genuine spirituality. I'm exaggerating, but not too much. The only thing that will bring about the change into a new age is that the earth is shaken, that we are shaken, and we are going to be shaken. We have already seen the beginning of it. You have to know not to be afraid. Only if you keep a very, very open channel, an open mind and no fear, will great insight and revelations come to you. They can happen to all of you [...] One way to not be afraid is to know

that death does not exist, that everything in this life has a positive purpose. Get rid of all your negativity and begin to view life
as a challenge, a testing ground of your own inner resources and
strength [...] You make your own hell or your own heaven by the
way you have lived.

Dr. Kubler-Ross was a psychiatrist. She was committed to address-
ing the needs of both the dying patient and his or her loved ones. Her
five stages of coping with the news of impending death have become
the standard by which those working with the dying approach the
patient. She was a scientist, not a faith-healer, and certainly not a mys-
tic. Only after she was confronted with story after story from those close
to death or who had recovered from a near-death experience did she
refocus her energies on what occurs at death.

Great scientists don't make the facts fit their hypotheses. They eval-
uate the data they obtain from experimentation and observation, and
use that data to formulate a new hypothesis. Dr. Kubler-Ross insists that
death is not the end but just the transition to what's next. She is certainly not the first to believe this, but her data—from many thousands
of patients—is compelling. What is most amazing to me are the clear
parallels between her discoveries and those of physicists like Einstein.
Dr. Kubler-Ross, like Einstein, is proclaiming that the world is not what
we think. However, she takes it a step further and proclaims that in fact
life *and* death are not what we think.

We will hear more from Dr. Kubler-Ross in the final section of this
book. In the next chapter we will see how her deductions mesh with
some theories presented by others, all of whom will be making the case
that the world is indeed not what you think.

chapter ten

COMMON THREADS

I t is often said that there are no new ideas under the sun. Don't tell that to the Wright brothers or for that matter to our friend Albert Einstein. There are indeed new ideas under the sun, but these are admittedly few and far between. Most of our ideas are recycled, but that does not make them less important. Recall from chapter eight that each of us is required to play the part we have been given regardless of how many times the same lines have already been recited.

Elizabeth Kubler-Ross, who we discussed in the previous chapter, was of course not the only person in history to notice some of the peculiarities of life and the universe that are the focus of this book. She had company, and among them were great scientists, philosophers, and thinkers. When the same idea repeatedly and independently reveals itself to many, it implies (but of course does not guarantee) that it may some represent some universal truth. Many of the concepts we have already discussed in this book have been described by others well before me. Over the next few pages I will quote a spectrum of authors and thinkers. You will recognize the themes, and I hope that you will be as struck as I am that these are people who have independently, and via disparate routes, arrived at some common conclusions.

We begin with the physician, thinker, and writer Deepak Chopra. Dr. Chopra, though classically trained in Western medicine, has roots in Indian medicine and has taught about the interconnection between mind and body. Author of many books on spirituality and the role of consciousness in the universe, Dr. Chopra has shared profound insights into the workings of the universe and our role within that universe. Below are a few quotes from his *Book of Secrets.*

The life you know is a thin layer of events covering a deeper reality..."

Ever since you and I were born, we've had a constant stream of clues hinting at another world insides ourselves.

Thanks to Einstein, we realize that we are embedded in nature; the observer changes reality by the very act of observation.

Most of us take for granted that time flies, meaning it passes too quickly. But in the mindful state, time doesn't really pass at all. There is only a single instant of time that keeps renewing itself over and over with infinite variety...In the one reality, the only time on the clock is now.

Let's begin with the first quote, that life is a thin layer covering a deeper reality. Dr. Chopra is telling us that what we see and what we experience are but a veneer. The real story of life, he teaches, lies beneath this surface and is waiting to be discovered by each of us. What is the real story of life? According to Dr. Chopra, each of our lives represents the power of creation, and our participation in life is no less than a continual process of creation. We make our own reality, all of it. You may recall that in chapter seven we discussed how every one of our decisions initiates a cascade of events. We have seen how the most simple decision—for example to make a left turn instead of a right turn—can change the lives of so many. In fact, with each decision the entire universe changes; we continually create reality. I think it fair to rephrase Dr. Chopra's quote; he is telling us that the world is not what we think.

Dr. Chopra then offers another statement, another concept we have touched upon already in this book beginning with our survey from chapter three. Clues, he insists, are everywhere, and they point to another world inside ourselves. He gives examples of these clues, such as the wonder we occasionally experience in nature, and he talks of how these clues inform us that life is more than it appears to be. He continues: "Countless clues have come your way, only to be overlooked because they didn't form a clear message." Throughout the first half of this book we have discussed a few of these clues. Dr. Chopra is correct; clues are everywhere. They are in our work, in our play, in all of our relationships and experiences. Part two of this book, *What The World Is*, will discuss this in detail.

When Dr. Chopra states that we are embedded in nature and that observations change reality, he is referencing quantum physics. We learned in chapter five that the observation of an event, such as measuring the path of a photon, changes the outcome of the event. Observation changes reality. This is an absolutely bizarre quantum truth that defies rational explanation. (Actually, it may in fact be rational but we don't yet possess the knowledge or insight to recognize its rationality.) Observations, even if they occur long after a decision is made (such as we saw in a variation of the double slit experiment), will change what occurred. The future, in some still-mysterious way, does affect the present. This is accurate; this is the way our world works.

Finally, Dr. Chopra references time. As we have also repeatedly discussed, our interpretation of time is based on an illusion. Dr. Chopra confirms this and references consciousness. While we are mindful—meaning consciously aware of the moment—time does not seem to pass at all. "There is only a single instant of time that keeps renewing itself over and over...the only time on the clock is now." This is a critical concept in understanding our world. Past and future are truly illusions. Each moment of time is perpetually alive; moments don't "die" and become the past.

Dr. Deborah Tannen, a socio-linguist from Georgetown University and author of multiple books, wrote an op-ed piece in the *Washington Post* (September 28, 2008), after the death of her father at age ninety-eight. During a college reunion she spotted an older-looking gentleman, and initially had no recollection of his identity. Suddenly, she recognized him as a friend from many years past:

> It was as if aging was a layer of makeup smeared upon his face—makeup that someone had just wiped off. I remembered then a conversation I'd had with my father when he was in his early

nineties. "Daddy," I asked, "what does it feel like to be old?" "I don't know," he replied. "I don't feel old. When I pass a mirror I think, who's that old man?"

My father's own sense of time was telescoped as he aged. Though he never lost his mental acuity or wit, he often remembered past events as more recent than they were. Toward the end of his life, he referred to his mother having died a few years before. I pointed out that she'd been dead for 33 years. "Thirty-three years?" he said in astonishment. "And she's still bugging me!"

In his last year of life, my father remarked, "When I'm walking along and thinking of people I knew, I think about them as if they're alive. Then I remember that they're dead."

Many would read those few sentences and assume that Dr. Tannen's father had a bit of dementia, perhaps Alzheimer's disease. I believe that this is a misinterpretation of what is occurring. Since all moments of time are permanent fixtures in the block that is space-time, it is not difficult to imagine recalling those moments in what appears to be random versus chronological order. As Dr. Kubler-Ross taught us in the last chapter, at death we can visit those who have passed long ago not at the age they should currently be but at the age we recall them. For some reason, as we approach the end of our life, we seem to get "confused" about the order of things. However, the order of moments is an illusion. The order is something that we have created to make sense of our existence, but it is only an illusion. All moments of time are equal, and so it is probably an advantage and in some ways a gift to be able to recall moments independently of time and to enjoy them as they are meant to be enjoyed. Does it matter if Dr. Tannen's grandmother died thirty-three or three years earlier? The memories that she engendered in her son are memories of their shared experiences; the order of occurrence is of little significance.

Recently I attended my thirty-fifth college reunion. My college friends, just as Dr. Tannen described her old friend at her reunion, looked like young actors wearing makeup so that they appeared to be old. My first thought—and I wasn't the only one feeling this way—was

"How in the world did we get here? How did this happen?" We all recalled days gone by—thirty-five years gone by, in fact—as if it had all happened just yesterday. But those memories weren't yesterday, they were "today." It is always today. The only reality is now. We just keep moving from one today to another, from one "now" to another, but those other nows don't disappear. Memory is more accurately a re-experiencing of a previous now.

Walter Isaacson, in his excellent book *Einstein*, references two of Albert Einstein's communications on this issue. In a letter to his friend the Queen Mother of Belgium, he offered the following: "The strange thing about growing old is that the intimate identification with the here and now is slowly lost. One feels transposed into infinity, more or less alone." What is this infinity that Einstein is trying to describe? It is the sense of leaving your current now, that placeholder that you occupy in time, and instead hovering over the entire loaf of space-time, as if you could reach down and pluck any one moment and relive it. Perhaps this is what occurs at or near death. More on this a bit later.

In another letter he sent to the family of his colleague Michele Besso after his good friend's passing, Einstein stated, "He has departed from this strange world a little ahead of me. That means nothing. For us believing physicists, the distinction between past, present and future is only a stubborn illusion."

Kurt Gödel was a brilliant mathematician who left Europe during World War II and became a professor at Princeton University at the time Einstein was also on the faculty. The two became good friends. According to Walter Isaacson in his book *Einstein*, Gödel was intrigued by the implications of Einstein's theory of special relativity, especially concerning our understanding of time. Gödel is quoted as saying:

> The existence of an objective lapse of time means that reality consists of an infinity of layers of 'now' which come into existence successively. But if simultaneity is something relative, each observer has his own set of "nows," and none of these various layers can claim the prerogative of representing the objective lapse of time.

In other words, since each of us experiences time differently depending on our relative state of motion, and since our recognition of simultaneity differs depending on that state of motion, there can be no absolute flow of time. Time does not flow. It seems to us as if it does; in fact, we would bet the ranch on it. We would lose. Time just is. One moment abuts another, yet that first moment never disappears. Pick your point in space-time; all moments exist at once.

Consider Hermann Hesse, a twentieth-century German author greatly influenced by his visits to India. His work *Siddhartha* is about the protagonist's search for enlightenment, a common Eastern theme. Hesse's take on the search for enlightenment is unique. Siddhartha learns that life is not chronological, but is instead a summation of one's experiences plus the acquisition of wisdom. The *order* in which experiences are acquired and wisdom earned is not important. In the latter portion of the book Siddhartha returns to a river which is part of a recurrent theme in the story. He tells us:

> ...I reviewed my life and it was also a river, and Siddhartha the boy, Siddhartha the mature man and Siddhartha the old man, were only separated by shadows, not through reality. Siddhartha's previous lives were also not in the past, and his death and his return to Brahma are not in the future. Nothing was, nothing will be, everything has reality and presence. Were not all difficulties and evil in the world conquered as soon as one conquered time, as soon as one dispelled time?

In that paragraph, Hesse is describing the block that is space-time, the totality of all moments that perpetually exist. At the conclusion of the book, Siddhartha adds:

> Time is not real, Govinda. I have realized this repeatedly. And if time is not real, then the dividing line that seems to lie between this world and eternity, between suffering and bliss, between good and evil, is also an illusion.

Einstein, Elizabeth Kubler-Ross, Hermann Hesse, Deepak Chopra, and so many others throughout history—impressive thinkers from markedly disparate cultures and disciplines—all arrived at the same conclusions. Time is not what we think. Reality is not what we assume. Our world is not what it appears to be.

These statements should no longer surprise you; the case has been made in these ten chapters. There can be no doubt that our world indeed works in mysterious ways, ways that are not random but in fact are exceedingly specific.

So what of it? Why does it matter, what do these clues reveal? What difference does it make to any of our lives? Short answer: it is the basis of *all* that matters. Once you agree that the world is not what you have assumed it to be, you must then ask the question, "What is this world?" If our world is but one out of an infinite number of possible worlds, then why this particular one? It implies a reason, it implies a purpose, it implies a point. Now let's get on with finding out just what that point is and the implications for our individual and collective existence. Here is a hint: we are out to change six billion lives and the fate of a planet.

PART II

WHAT THE WORLD IS

chapter eleven

THERE IS NO PIE

We have made the case: the world is not what we think. As I stated at the end of the last chapter, once you accept that fact, you must then ask, "If it's not what we thought, then what *is* this world?" This world of ours is a bizarre place, a collage of incredible moments of love and beauty, and unfortunately also moments of terror and tragedy. It is a world where no one actually wins, since even the most wealthy and powerful return to the dust. It is a place where death is inevitable, no matter how hard we try to avoid it. It is a place of magic, where water freezes at just the right temperature and gravity is just so, where flowers know just when to bloom and leaves know just when to fall, where night and day arrive like clockwork and winter begets spring every single year. This world is anything but random.

To these facts we add some new ones we have now come to accept. Time and space behave in a ghostly manner (chapter four). All events are just the singular outcome of infinite quantum possibilities. The future affects the past as much as the converse (chapter five). Add in the soft clues we uncovered in chapters six through ten, and we are ready to answer some fascinating questions:

(1) Is there a "best" or "right" life?

(2) What, or who, is really family? Is there more to the concept of family than meets the eye?

(3) What are we to make of the ubiquity of violence? Must it always be so? Is there any hope for us to even imagine a world without violence?

(4) What is the true currency of life? What should we be earning and saving?

(5) If we actually can decipher a purpose to life, what implications does it have for the way we live?

"Life is a zero-sum game." It's a common statement and a well known one, and it implies that there are fixed amounts of resources in this world. In order for me to prosper, someone—perhaps you—must suffer. Increasing my portion decreases the amount available to everyone else. It is to say that each of us must fight for our "market share." Whatever accrues to me means that less is available to you. There is only so much pie.

It is quite logical to assume that there is a pie with a fixed size. Who would believe that there is an unlimited supply of diamonds or oil on this planet? No one, so we extrapolate and assume that everything is in limited supply. That would include happiness. This is because we assume that happiness is in some way proportional to what we individually possess. Even if you personally don't agree with that statement, collectively this is precisely how we behave. We fiercely attempt to collect wealth and power. We drool over a wide array of material goods, and we covet stations or positions in life. There is no doubt that most of us focus on personally obtaining as large a portion of the limited resources on the planet as possible. According to the theory of life as a zero-sum game, anytime your slice of those limited resources increases—whether it's money, jewels, or power—my slice is diminished. I will, by definition, have less since you have more, and if happiness is proportional to what each of us possesses, more for you simply means that my happiness is lessened.

We act as if the pie is fixed, and we compete openly and brazenly for our slice. For most of us, however, it is clear that more is in play. Our survey from chapter three demonstrated that a good number of us sense that something greater exits, something beyond those tangible resources which are in limited supply. President Barack Obama, in his book *The Audacity of Hope,* describes this phenomenon:

Each day, it seems, thousands of Americans are going about their daily rounds—dropping off the kids at school, driving to the office, flying to a business meeting, shopping at the mall, trying to stay on their diets—and coming to the realization that something is missing.

They are deciding that their work, their possessions, their diversions, their sheer busyness are not enough. They want a sense of purpose, a narrative arc to their lives, something that will relieve a chronic loneliness or lift them above the exhausting, relentless toll of daily life. They need an assurance that somebody out there cares about them, is listening to them—that they are not just destined to travel down a long highway toward nothingness.

President Obama was discussing the importance of religion in America in the above excerpt and explaining why it was inseparable from both the history of America and the governing of the nation. Religion does offer solace for billions, and it satisfies that thirst for an explanation of our lives. Of course along with the noble aspects of religion, we also have those thorny issues of fanaticism, the unending conflicts among the believers of various religions, and the unspeakable violence and cruelty too often practiced in religion's name. What we really want is a solution that provides the required comfort and the explanations that religion can offer, but without those undesirable side effects.

Competing books alternately castigate and promote religion. Atheists point out those significant negatives mentioned above and make the case that religion does far more harm than good to humanity. Their mantra: human reason needs to triumph over myth. Of course the problem is that so far human reason has failed miserably. Without religion, or more accurately without a deity, setting standards of behavior becomes more problematic. Whose opinion holds sway, mine or yours? Without invoking some higher authority, we are left with one individual's opinion against another. This type of opinion contest is usually settled with whatever weapon happens to exist at the particular time in history the argument occurs.

Religion's proponents have made the same case for centuries. We exist to serve God. The Word or the Book is all we need. Have faith in

God and the world to come. To that the following reply is frequently offered: "Great, but what about the mess in *this* world, the one that we live in?" Don't worry, we are assured. It's just temporary. Yes, temporary, but for many quite painful. As we are all too aware, the Word—and just what that Word is varies from religion to religion—is far too often used as a blunt instrument to oppress or defeat those who believe otherwise.

As long as we continue to accept that the world we see is the world that is, we are forever stuck in this merry-go-round of argument. No one opinion will ever triumph; this war of ideas will be waged for eternity, and with it will come more of the same kinds of unpleasantness that we have witnessed since man set foot on Earth. The clues we have uncovered offer a different path, a way out of this maze. Since the world is clearly not what we thought it to be, we are no longer constrained by what seems to be its reality. Physics has proven without any doubt whatsoever that the reality we presume to be real is just an illusion. How could the future affect the present or even the past (the way it unquestionably does) in the reality we "know?" It can't. The reality we know is a smokescreen, a diversion from the reality that is.

The world we know, of course, seems quite real to us. We feel real pain and sorrow, we feel joy. Objects respond as we would expect them to, not in some weird quantum way. But we have proven without a doubt that what we see and experience is just a fraction of what is, and in fact the deductions we make from our senses are misleading when it comes to understanding how the world actually works.

The beliefs to which we cling are no different. They are based on our distorted interpretation of reality. Why is this important? Once we realize that the world is quite different than is commonly imagined, we become free to cast off those erroneous beliefs which have mired us in this rut of repetitive and destructive human behavior. Recall from chapter one the options for explaining the world. Option three proposed that we have chronically misinterpreted the world. Part one of this book has hopefully convinced you that this is so.

Which beliefs are we to discard, and to which should we cling? That is the first step in discovering the real world, not the world of illusion in which we find ourselves. We have spent ten chapters uncovering clues that will help us make this determination. We need only take a close look at them to answer this question.

We begin with the title of this chapter—there is no pie. This idea of limited resources and competition for those limited resources is a primary source of contentiousness in the world. There is in fact no pie, or at least no pie of fixed size. This entire concept of competing for precious resources is based on the assumption that a winning life is determined by our station in life, by the amount of dollars or trophies we have accumulated, or by the number of individuals that can recognize our face. If the purpose of life is to achieve great wealth or fame, then competing for the largest possible piece of the pie is absolutely rational. But we already know that to be incorrect. That is because the essence of life has nothing at all to do with accumulating anything material. Death takes care of that issue.

Honey bees are a miraculous lot. They work and work and work. There is but one queen per colony; the rest are drones who follow directions. Bees do not individually progress. Generation after generation, bees perform the same tasks. No lifetime achievement awards are available, no lifelong friendships are created and nurtured. What is the point of a honey bee's life? Work hard, build the hive, serve the queen. No drone will ever ascend to the throne of the queen, no matter how reliable and industrious that individual is. Born a drone, die a drone.

Not so with humans. We can progress and grow, we can strive and achieve. We can forge innumerable friendships and relationships in the years we are granted. We can fall in love, we can share experiences with our friends and families, and we can become something more today than we were yesterday. We are unique among species in this regard.

Christians speak of free will, the privilege granted humans to make of their own lives what they choose. According to the doctrine of free will, each of us has license to pursue whichever path we choose, good or evil. Only if free will exists can God hold us responsible for our actions and fairly judge us. If instead all of our actions are predetermined, or predestined, we can hardly be responsible for our choices. But free will is actually much more than this. It is an enormous opportunity, a gift given to each of us. It is what differentiates us from the remainder of Earth's occupants.

We talked in an earlier chapter about the imaginary pyramid of life. Most of us liken our journey through the years to the ascent of a pyramid, with personal victory represented by a successful path to its zenith. Here we confront one of those beliefs we need to shed, because it is born of the fictitious reality we observe. It assumes there is a "right" or a "best" life. Perhaps you have a friend who epitomizes this right life. She is smart and beautiful, successful in both career and personal relationships, and has always been so. Hers, it would seem, is the right life, or at the minimum the preferred life.

Not only is there no fixed-size pie, there is no right or best or preferred life. How do I know this? I know this from the clues we have uncovered earlier. Perhaps the most critical clue of all is the fragility and finiteness of life. No matter your accomplishments or lack of such, no matter your station in life, and no matter if you are powerless or the most powerful, life is finite and you will die. And when you die, all of your assets, financial and otherwise, immediately revert to zero worth, at least as far as you, the deceased, is concerned. All that remains is the influence you have had on the lives of others. We have two clues here. That your asset value returns immediately to zero is clue one, which we will discuss here. Clue two involves your impact on the lives of others. This clue deserves, and will receive, a chapter of its own.

We live and die no matter who we are. One cannot differentiate one life from another on the basis of creation and death; all lives experience both. There is no winning or losing. No matter how you have spent your moments on Earth, death is your prize. For the purposes of our current discussion, the fact that death is always the final word is sufficient to make the case that all lives have at least some level of equivalence. "Some level of equivalence," however, is insufficient to prove that there is no preferred life. For this we need to revisit a few more clues. Recall our discussion of the creation of reality from chapter eight. Each of us creates reality by the force of even our most simple choices. To quote directly from chapter eight, choice equals reality. There are no adjectives or modifiers in this equation. This equation does not state that good or clever or educated choices are better than foolish or ignorant choices. Every single choice initiates a cascade of events that produces the reality we experience. The universe unfolds differently depending on our choices, but it always unfolds; it cannot be stopped. Reality has no net worth; it just is. No one reality is preferred over another as far as the universe is concerned, and no one choice is preferred.

There is no question that it is difficult to accept the statement that all choices are equal to the universe, but nevertheless, it is true. History advances no matter the events that transpire. Acts of loving kindness do not affect the universe any differently than heinous acts of murder and wanton destruction. Our universe cares not a bit whether you make choices that are better for yourself or for the earth, or if you instead make idiotic decisions. Success and failure are human terms; the universe cares nothing about such nouns.

From the perspective of the unfolding of the universe, all choices are equal, all events are equal, and all moments are equal (since there is no actual flow of time). Understand that one is not relieved of personal responsibility because of this fact of nature, because although the universe cares nothing about what transpires in the course of time, the choices you make while you are alive count very much indeed. While this seems paradoxical, it is not. Every life, and every moment of every life, is equivalent in terms of base value to the universe. No moment or life is preferred. There is no right life or best life—not from the point of view of totality. What gives a life value is what it contributes to the lives of others. We will talk about that just ahead.

An unfolding universe. This is the image that is required to best illustrate why there is no preferred life. In 1968, Robert Kennedy was poised to become President of the United States. He was about to receive the Democratic nomination for President and would likely have defeated Richard Nixon in the general election. Of course, minutes after winning the California primary—a giant leap towards securing both of those electoral victories—Robert Kennedy was murdered. U.S. history would almost assuredly have been different had he lived and won the election. The Vietnam war may have ended years earlier, and lives on both sides may have been saved. Watergate would never have occurred.

Of course we have no way of knowing what other events, positive and negative, might have accompanied a Kennedy presidency.

What we do know is that regardless of whether Robert Kennedy was or was not murdered, or whether he did or did not become the President of the United States, just about everyone who was sixty years of age or older in 1968 would no longer be alive today. We know that today's fashions would likely be the same, today's weather would be unaffected, climate change would still be an issue, and the winning and losing football teams of the past forty years would probably have not been reversed.

In other words, the universe and our world would have still unfolded. This unfolding is unstoppable, regardless of who is President or what any of us does, no matter what choices are made. Everyone makes decisions—every one of us makes dozens of choices daily. To the universe, those choices are completely irrelevant; the universe will unfold either way. For this reason, there is no right or best or even preferred choice, and in turn no right or best or preferred life. Not only will the universe not be affected by any single choice, the fact of our death will not change. Any single choice or decision can certainly affect the date of a person's death, but not the fact that death will be our fate.

The significance of this concept—an equivalence of all moments and of all choices and actions, and therefore of all lives—cannot be overstated. It means that all existence is relevant, all life worthwhile, and most critically that all lives contribute equally to the unfolding of the universe. One cannot be born into an impossible situation. No level of poverty or deprivation minimizes a life. No amount of turmoil or angst minimizes a life. No lack of opportunity minimizes a life. This is what the reality of our universe is telling us.

It is also telling us that since every one of us is participating equally in the creation of reality, the fuel of creation must be something obtainable for all, not just a select few. What drives the world and determines the value of a life must be something in limitless supply. Wealth and power are just the opposite, available in limited supply to a miniscule minority, and therefore cannot be the essential elements to defining a life. Wealth and power also evaporate instantaneously at death; they are a distraction from the real game.

Our clues point to something much more complex than a simple climb up the face of a pyramid. We have repeatedly witnessed the incredibly precise design of nature. Time seemingly advances, yet nothing changes in this world. History is repeated again and again. We learn little as we advance through time; we are plagued by the same issues generation after generation. We begin life ignorant and remain that way for decades, by which time we have made countless personal mistakes, echoing the stories of the millions who have come before us.

These are powerful clues that something else is afoot. Wealth and power wax and wane. Fabulously wealthy and powerful individuals have cyclically inhabited the planet, and to what end? We have repeatedly witnessed the fall of the powerful and the sorrow and emptiness that haunt so many of the wealthy. Clearly life's secret does not lie in either of these. What we really want to know is this. If money and power are not the true currency of life, then what is?

chapter twelve

THE CURRENCY
OF LIFE

I magine a trip to the supermarket. You fill your cart with groceries and head for the checkout line. The cashier picks up the carton of milk, scans it, and the computer screen comes up blank. She tries the eggs, then the bananas and the whole-grain bread. Same result. "I'm sorry," she says. "Your items can't be scanned." Puzzled, you pick up your groceries and look them over. "Why not?" you inquire. "I can see the bar codes." "Yes," she answers, "but there is no specific value associated with those bar codes. I don't know if I should charge you in dollars or euros, shiny rocks or beads."

Society collectively decides on a value system for the transfer of goods and services. Over the centuries, this has evolved from the direct trade of one food for another, then to more generalized barter, and eventually to a system using an agreed-upon currency such as gold or printed money. Without such a system, trade is severely restricted, which is what still happens when economies sink and trust in the value of the agreed-upon currency is diminished.

In real life when the cashier scans your groceries, he knows that in the United States a number with a dollar sign will appear on the electronic display; he doesn't think twice about the type of currency that you must present in order to take home those groceries. Money, whether it's in the form of cash or a check or a credit card, is the currency of trade. This concept of currency transcends the purchase of goods and services; there is an implied currency behind much of what we do. For example, flowers and gifts, whispered words of affection, and our undistracted attention are the currency of romance. Quid pro quos and outright bribes are too often the currency of politics. Since in this book we are in search of the purpose of life, we need to identify the currency of life. Why? Because without knowing just what that currency is, we are without direction in our attempt to maximize the value of life.

When we think of the currency of trade, we understand that we will need to acquire, save, and efficiently employ that currency—dollars, euros, and so on—to maximize our ability to successfully trade for goods and services. The currency of life is no different. We must decide how to acquire, save, and efficiently employ that currency to make our lives more valuable. Of course none of this is possible until we know just what that currency is. So the next step is to review our clues and see if we can identify that currency.

Movie stars, athletes, politicians, and the very rich are envied and pursued. Why do the paparazzi chase down the rich and famous? Supply and demand: photos of these individuals sell. They sell because we the public want to see them—we want to follow even the most mundane aspects of these peoples' lives. As we scan their stories and photos, we imagine ourselves to be their friends and confidants. This "relationship" increases our own personal sense of worth, foolish as that is.

More is involved in this chase after the stars. We collectively make a value statement as we pursue this intimacy with these beautiful people. Fame and fortune are what attracts us; fame and fortune are what we seek. Greater fame or fortune means more influence, more fringe benefits, more overall importance. What this pursuit of the rich and famous implies is that fame and fortune are the currency of life.

Of course this is no startling revelation. Money has historically been the currency of life, in whatever form that money may take. It doesn't matter if it is earned or inherited, fairly or unfairly—we don't seem to differentiate. Fortune is fortune; it garners our admiration and often our envy. We assume that the wealthy are just smarter than the rest of us, that they have some sort of magical wisdom that transcends their particular expertise—if they even have one—and generalizes into many arenas of life. There is little reason to assume that Hollywood stars have some great insight into solving world or national problems, but they are the people we hear responding to such questions on TV and radio. Fame begets fortune and fortune begets privilege and status, which in turn create power. It would seem there is no argument to be made here; fame and fortune are the accepted currency of life.

Jean Paul Sartre, the existentialist philosopher whom we briefly discussed in chapter two, penned the following:

> Life is nothing until it is lived; but it is yours to make sense of, and the value of it is nothing else but the sense that you choose.

This is no small statement, because it in effect refutes the argument that fame and fortune are necessarily the currency of life. It doesn't claim that they aren't; in fact, it does not specify any specific currency of life. "The value of it is nothing else but the sense that you choose." Each of us, according to Sartre, gets to decide what life is worth, and therefore we also choose the currency of life. Existentialist philosophy proclaims that each life is a blank slate without any defined purpose— existence before essence. Each individual may make of his life what he chooses. Therefore he defines his own purpose and in turn his own currency of life.

Jean Paul Sartre was born in 1905, the year Einstein published his three famous scientific papers, including the paper describing his theory of special relativity. The existentialists, including Sartre, may not have had the benefit of understanding the significance of Einstein's explanation of time and space or the implications of quantum physics, which we have identified as major clues in our pursuit of life's purpose. These clues contradict Sartre's theory that the purpose of life is individually defined. While we have seen that each of us does in fact create reality with our choices, this is distinct from the act of personally defining the purpose of life. On the contrary, many of the clues we have discussed speak to a universality of life's purpose:

- We don't learn from our mistakes. Generation after generation commits the same foolish errors, individually and collectively.

■ Humans have not effectively evolved. We still kill each other and we still create——only to eventually destroy.

■ We age, and our interests and perspective change. As we have discussed previously, this implies a universal purpose to the stages of life. We could have been programmed differently so that our interests and perspective remained fixed.

■ Our world is but one world out of an infinite number of possible worlds. It need not be this particular way. But it is this way, with characteristics that permit life as we know it.

These clues suggest that, contrary to existentialist doctrine, we do not individually determine life's meaning. We are free to explore and experience life in a very personal manner, but the themes of life precede our arrival. Sartre and the other existentialists were partially correct in their thesis and conclusions:

(1) Existence does precede essence.

(2) We indeed create our own reality with our choices.

(3) We are each responsible for the course of our lives.

(4) There are no external excuses.

Life, however, is not in itself the purpose of our presence on Earth as they would have us believe. While we are here to live a life, a full and creative life, there is far more at play than simple existence. If the sole point of our existence on this earth involved living whatever life we choose and then individually deciding the purpose of that life, our world would be quite different. If no overarching theme underpinned human existence, that specific set of features unique to our universe and to our humanness would neither be required nor present. We would not be "stuck" in our current human condition. We would not need to age, and our perspectives would not change as we age. We would evolve in such a way that intelligent people would preferentially survive and prosper, leading ultimately to a more cerebral population—which by itself would secure greater happiness and longevity.

We would not make the same mistakes over and over again as a species or as individuals.

In a world governed solely by evolution and chemistry, we might expect *these* predictable results—not the rather weird set of circumstances that we do find as we identify and examine our clues. In such a random and purely physical world, death would be the absolute end. But we are beginning to understand that death may very well not be the end. The common concept of death that most of us share is likely erroneous, much more illusion than reality. As we have already learned from Albert Einstein, Elizabeth Kubler-Ross, and others, death may not be what we have traditionally presumed it to be.

I used to think that living, or more accurately surviving, was above all else the critical goal. That is, no matter the cost, we should strive to survive. After all, if we are gone we can do nothing, accomplish nothing, and learn nothing. Being courageous and heroic was foolhardy if it meant significant risk of death—a living coward beats a dead hero. Stay alive as long as possible; that's the mission. But I missed the point. I mistakenly believed, as did the existentialists, that life itself was the point.

As a physician, I see many elderly patients filled with anxiety, men and women waiting to find out if the latest medical test I have just performed has uncovered some dreadful issue that would mean that their lives would soon end.

A woman of eighty-five years sits before me, consumed with the possibility that there is something terribly wrong with her. "Mrs. King," I assure her, "all of your tests are fine. I haven't found any problem. Except one."

"What is the problem?" she asks, almost catatonic as she awaits my reply.

"You are eighty-five and still in good health. Every minute you waste by frantically worrying about the next possible medical catastrophe subtracts from the time you have to enjoy life."

The great irony, I explain to her, is that she is in effect already dead. That her worst fear—that she will die—has already come true, since she is certainly not living. Not as long as she is consumed with dread about what may occur.

Life itself is not the goal; living a meaningful life is. If you have sacrificed yourself for another or for a noble cause, you likely have fulfilled your mission and have lived a successful life, no matter the length. Of course the cause must not be frivolous—a life is nothing to waste—but life itself is not the goal. That is the same reason that fame and wealth cannot be the goals. As we have already seen, both revert to zero at death. Nothing of value remains if money and recognition is all that there was to a particular life.

Power is no different than fame and fortune; it is just as transient. And actually, it detracts from a life rather than enhancing it. The most powerful people are often sealed off from others. Relationships become much harder to develop and nurture and so they tend to be asymmetric, unbalanced—they have little depth. The less powerful partner in that relationship is to some degree subservient to the more powerful person, which diminishes the benefits of that relationship for both.

Fame, fortune, and power are without a doubt not the currency of life. Clearly neither is the number of days we live; longevity alone delivers nothing of value. Just as our eighty-five-year-old woman wastes her days consumed with the fear of a future she is already living, so too do many of us waste countless days in pursuit of empty goals. Whether we spend one year or one hundred years chasing the illusions of fame, fortune, and power is irrelevant. One's total number of days on this earth is a meaningless statistic unless those days are spent accumulating and wisely spending the real currency of life.

What is the currency of life? The currency of life is love.

We assume we know what love is, but for our purpose in this book we need to clearly define what we mean by that term. Love is not the same as passion. It is not solely that tingly feeling you get when you are falling in love or are infatuated with another. Love is what results from the development of and the investment in interpersonal relationships, the positive interactions that we have with others. Love is of course what we feel for family and friends—two sides of the same coin, as we will see shortly. Love, however, can also be what we learn to feel by becoming engaged at just about any level with many other people, some of whom are complete strangers.

Here is the key to assimilating this most important concept. By now I hope you understand and accept that we are all inextricably linked together in the creation of reality. Since there are no unimportant moments and since everyone's choices and decisions equally create reality, we are all continuously participating in the unfolding of the universe and therefore in the unfolding of each of our lives. Those artificial concepts that tend to segregate and separate us—culture, religion, and heritage—are but further illusions, and they too often prevent us from recognizing the truth of our collective and shared existence. Once the light goes on and you realize that this is precisely the way the world works—that we equally and collectively create reality—it becomes natural to begin to love each other simply because we are so interdependent and interrelated, and because we're inseparable.

The currency of life is love, and it manifests in acts of assistance, in helping others. And not just for the benefit of those people themselves, but equally for the self-satisfaction and personal growth it provides. It is manifested when we are kind and generous, loyal and forgiving, empathetic and compassionate. Love, the real currency of life, is the result of thousands of individual interpersonal interactions. As we pass through this life, what we need to save and spend wisely is love, in all of the ways just described.

Why am I absolutely certain that this is so? Those clues we have repeatedly revisited confirm that our world is not what we think, and they testify to the hidden reality behind the fact of our existence. Remember that every moment is equivalent to every other, and that every choice and decision initiates a cascade of events, all of which contribute to the reality in which we find ourselves. We *all* participate in the universe, and we do so equally. No one is excluded; no single choice or decision is preferred to another no matter how powerful, wealthy, poor, or ignorant the decider. This is not some liberal or egalitarian statement, the metaphysical equivalent to the idea that every player on a youth athletic team should receive a trophy. We have seen how each and every decision, choice, and action immediately spawns a chain of events that creates reality, no matter the status of the creator. If the currency of life were power or money, the asymmetry of life would preclude the involvement of the majority. Only a tiny fraction of the earth's population will every have very much of either. The currency of life cannot be fame, fortune, or power; too many would be excluded, and the universe does not permit this option. Every choice and decision by every conscious creature must be counted, and they are all in play. This is not opinion; this is the way the universe works.

No matter your station on this earth, all of us have the opportunity to create relationships. We can all have friends towards whom we can be caring and loyal. We can all lend a hand or an ear to one in need. We can all dedicate ourselves to making the world better for another in even the smallest ways. That is one way we know that the real currency of life is associated with our interaction with others; love is available to everyone equally, everywhere, and in every moment. This the universe demands.

But there is another even more obvious clue that illustrates the fact that love is the currency of life. During 2008 and 2009, for example, an avalanche of the rich and powerful fell from their pedestals. These included the governors of two states, innumerable financial figures—including bank CEOs and famous investors—religious leaders, and sports figures. The list goes on and on. All tumbled and were humbled. Routinely, the rich and famous fall. As we mentioned earlier, if there were no purpose to life then once someone had reached the zenith they would be anointed victor. There would be no fall from grace. The trumpets would blare, a coronation would take place, and that would be that. Of course, that is not what occurs. What goes up often comes careening right back down.

While this crescendo and decrescendo of the rich and famous is occurring, there are inevitably other stories happening concurrently. These are stories of loyalty and love, of someone standing by another, of a generous hand helping the hopeless ascend. With every tragedy comes some glimmer of hope and some example of selflessness and incredible love. And what happens at such moments? Both the receiver and giver are lifted up; they are illuminated by the light of human goodness and kindness. As we shed a tear for some loss or marvel at the callousness of someone who had it all and should have known better, we inevitably shed a second tear at some simultaneous example of compassion. At every moment of every day, someone is touching another. Someone is lifting someone else's sorrow or drying someone else's tear. Someone is feeding the hungry or sheltering the homeless. These acts of loving kindness never cease. They are a constant on planet Earth.

This lesson could not be clearer. Fame and fortune—available to few and so frequently transient and empty—are shunned by the universe. Fame and fortune are too rare to be relevant. But love, in all of its manifestations, is embraced by the universe, for each loving act triggers a cascade as more love and more creativity envelop one person after another. It is a chain reaction that never ends, and one that enhances and expands the universe.

Too many of us have either missed or ignored the fact that love is the driving force of the universe. It is unquestionably the currency of life.

chapter thirteen

FAMILY

I was thirteen when I took my first airplane trip. Our flight left New York's JFK airport around noon on a clear January day. Eastern Pennsylvania was the farthest west I had ever been up to that moment of my life. My small world extended only as far as my neighborhood on Long Island and the five boroughs of New York City; I was completely urbanized. We bought everything we ate except the huge beefsteak tomatoes my father grew in his small patch of earth in our backyard.

As the plane headed west and the skyline of New York City receded in the distance, I began to realize that the world outside the boundaries of New York was far different than I had imagined. As we crossed into rural Pennsylvania, I was struck by the patchwork appearance of the ground below. What could explain the strange topography rolling on beneath our jet? My father must have sensed my confusion. He leaned over and pointed at the terrain below. "Those are farms. Most are square or rectangular, because that is how the crops are arranged, row upon row. One farm appears distinct from the next from up here because the rows are oriented differently on each, and different crops have a different appearance."

For this city boy, the view below was mesmerizing. I thought of little else for the duration of our flight, but once we landed in Ohio and met my mother's family in the terminal, I quickly forgot about the patchwork quilt of farms we had over flown. It wasn't until many years later on another flight over the Midwest that I once again marveled at the juxtaposition of farms in the heartland. This time I was struck by a much different thought. Each patch of the visual quilt represented a unique farm with a unique family inhabiting that farm. Each family had specific habits and customs which could be very different from those of another family living on another patch that I'd seen twenty minutes and hundreds of miles earlier. For each family on each patch, the world was specific and unique. Each had its own favorite foods, each a favorite song and a favorite movie. Each celebrated holidays in its own unique way, and each had a time to rise and a time to retire each day.

"Hi, we're the Mills family," is how Mr. Mills, the owner of one farm, might greet you upon your arrival. "Welcome to our farm. This is my father, Grandpa Mills, whose father—my grandfather—started this farm eighty years ago. Over on the porch is my mother—we just call her Grandma—and talking with her is my wife Sally. Somewhere around here are my four kids, and of course there's also our dog Scotty."

Mr. Mills's initial statement is what we might expect from any father introducing his flock. "We're the Mills family." What exactly does that mean? It simply expresses a genetic connection that unites the group we just met. A great grandfather has a child, now known as Grandpa, who along with Grandma has a son who marries Sally and has four offspring. Hardly news. Yet as I hope you might appreciate after twelve chapters, much of what we take for granted in life is more complex than it appears on the surface. Family is one of those concepts that is far more interesting than we might surmise.

The past fifty or so years have seen a remarkable advance in our understanding of genetics. DNA, deoxyribonucleic acid, is the software of life. DNA is a chemical blueprint for constructing all of the fundamental components of our bodies, and equally as important, it is a detailed set of instructions determining which cells should perform which functions in which particular order. The information portion of DNA resides in the amazingly creative structure of this molecule. DNA is composed of a central skeleton on which hang billions of chemical compounds called bases. Only four bases exist, yet when mixed in different order these bases comprise the entire genetic alphabet. They are the "letters" that spell out the words known as genes, which determine pretty much everything about how we are made and how we function.

DNA resides in the nucleus, the central island of each cell, and is formed into very long pieces of genetic material called chromosomes. Humans have twenty-three pairs of chromosomes—forty six chromosomes in all—and collectively these chromosomes contain about 24,000 genes. The total number of base pairs in the human genome—the term for the totality of all the DNA in those 24,000 genes—is over three billion. So those three billion base pairs, of which there are only four varieties, collectively spell out who we are.

Most of us are well aware of the controversy concerning the validity of the theory of evolution, which was posited by Charles Darwin in the nineteenth century. Evolution is actually the changing, or mutation, of DNA from its existing state to another state. The actual mechanism behind mutation is not complex. One or more of those three billion bases that hang off the backbone of DNA is replaced by a different base. Recall that there are only four possible bases in DNA. A mutation is a substitution of one of the four bases for another. It is equivalent to changing the letter "r" in the word "read" to a "d," which changes the word to "dead." One letter substituted for another, and we have a completely different meaning. One base change means different instructions for the cell, so either an important protein is not made correctly or at all—DNA is the instruction sheet for making proteins—or another is made in its place. Either way, the function of the cell is altered.

Some mutations are good. In evolutionary theory, those characteristics of organisms that increase the likelihood of survival will be "selected," meaning these will be passed along from one generation to the next. So if a random change of one or more bases in DNA occurs and results in a better situation for that species than before the change, over time that change will become permanent in DNA and that new, more successful trait will be passed on to following generations. Those mutations that are less helpful and diminish the odds of survival will be lost over time.

Other mutations are harmful and lead to diseases like hemophilia, a problem with blood clotting. Still others create problems with digestion or with the utilization of nutrients, which can lead to poor or absent growth or even death. Many examples of specific mutations exist, and there are undoubtedly countless more yet to be discovered. Mutation is a double-edged sword; sometimes it produces wonderful advantages for a species, while other times it leads to disease and even death.

Evidence for evolution is everywhere in nature. Perhaps the most fundamental evidence lies in DNA itself. DNA takes the same form in worms as it does in humans; all DNA, no matter where it is found in nature, is composed of the same skeleton and the same base pairs. The only difference is in the actual number and composition of genes, the number and order of base pairs. There is no doubt that evolution, the progression of species from one to the next, is very real. The evidence from DNA itself is indisputable. We are unquestionably related to many earlier forms of life. This fact alone, however, neither refutes nor supports the belief in a deity. As we have already witnessed, it is quite difficult to ignore all of the clues which together point to a lack of randomness in nature. Arguing against evolution is not only foolish, it is irrelevant if the point one is trying to make is that the world is more than a chemistry experiment. We already have plenty of evidence to the contrary.

Not only are we related to even the earliest forms of life in terms of our DNA, but we are closely related to each other as well. Each human cell contains DNA (except red blood cells, which have none). As mentioned above, about three billion base pairs are present in that DNA, encoding about 24,000 genes. Out of those three billion base pairs coding for those 24,000 genes, you and I have about 99 percent in common. That means that we share roughly 2,970,000,000 bases and 23,760 genes. Of course, the thirty million bases and two hundred forty genes that are distinct among us are not insignificant; we are of course different from one another.

Let's say we take some of your DNA and some from your brother, and while we are at it we take some from the person that you like least in the world. About 1 percent of your genes would be different from both—a few more would be like your brother's than your enemy's. We would have a hard time differentiating your brother from your enemy except in a few specific ways; for the most part they would look a lot alike. Extrapolating a bit, imagine the genetic differences between a Muslim and a Jew, or an Irish Protestant and an Irish Catholic, or a Shia and a Sunni. Except for the presence of a specific disease-causing mutation or two, you would be hard pressed to notice any difference at all. In fact, it would be impossible to decide with any certainty who was what.

Dr. Seuss was way ahead of geneticists. His story "Sneetches" is about typically creative Dr. Seuss characters, some of whom have a star on their belly and some who do not, The two groups are otherwise indistinguishable. Those who have a star are the elite, while those who don't are looked down upon as lacking. It's a story of discrimination that takes us on a wonderful journey as another Seussian character who owns a special machine enters the picture. For a fee, his machine can put a star on those starless Sneetches so that they can join the elite. When the original starred Sneetches realize they are losing their status, they are willing to pay even more to have their stars removed and once again look unique. Of course, this exchange between the starred and the starless runs rampant until one can no longer differentiate one Sneetch from another, which of course is his point. Substitute the ethnic and religious adversaries of our time for Dr. Seuss's Sneetches, and it's pretty apparent how ridiculous it all is.

We can take this further. Let's extract some DNA from Mr. Mills, Grandpa and Grandma Mills, and each of the four Mills children (we'll leave out Scotty the dog for the time being). We'll compare their DNA to the DNA of you and your family. You likely have already guessed that the differences would be quite minor. The Mills children would share a few more genes with Mom and Dad than they would with you, but the difference would be minimal. The Mills family, at least genetically, is barely distinguishable from countless other families.

So far we have met four generations of the Mills family: the great-grandfather who founded the farm, Grandpa, Mr. Mills, and the children. We can go farther back along the genealogical tree to identify the great-great-grandparents, then the great-great-great grandparents, and so on. Where should we stop our retrograde genealogic pursuit? How many generations? Where is the appropriate cutoff, the point at which the Mills family is diluted sufficiently to no longer consider it one family? Whom we should include in our family is not so clear. No specific delineating point is obvious, and of course if we keep going back far enough we would likely arrive at Adam, who you can accept as real or as the metaphor for a common progenitor.

Leaving genetics for just a paragraph, we need to take a closer look at just *what* we are. Each of us is composed of matter. The basic components of matter were created at or just after the origin of the universe, the Big Bang, and since matter cannot be created or destroyed, we are all approximately fourteen billion years old, which is the age of the universe. We are composed of atoms, protons and electrons, and their smaller component parts. We are not "new." We are all just recycled material. We have all been a part of stars and comets and other celestial bodies, as well as a part of everything and everyone who came before. Some of your current atomic components were once part of someone else, someone you never knew, someone not on your recent genealogical tree. What could possibly make two people closer than sharing atoms? We always were, and we always will be.

Genetic discoveries have changed our understanding of the world. We will soon be able to individually tailor medical treatments. Medications will be designed for one person's specific illness, whether it is an infectious or inherited disease or cancer. Unimaginable advances in all areas of life will become possible thanks to genetic research, advances that will improve and prolong life and raise the standard of living for millions. But the unraveling of the genetic code tells us something even more amazing: we are barely different; we are all related.

So if DNA is so similar among all people, then what differentiates us? If Mom and Dad give us DNA that is minutely different than someone from the other side of the world, what does that say about our identity? Clearly we are much more than our DNA; our personalities are forged to a very large degree in response to the environment. Our experiences matter. But the question then becomes, what makes us "family?"

What makes us family are shared experiences, shared values, and shared habits. These are acquired entities, not inherited. What this exercise in DNA and genes demonstrates is that family is far more about *relationship* than biology. In fact, the biology part represents an infinitesimal part of the equation that describes a family. Family is nothing more than whomever we deem to be family. Blood, in fact, is not really a whole lot thicker than water. If the relationships among family members are weak due to a whole host of factors, then blood—and by this I mean the few genes which family members share—is pretty much irrelevant. Anyone who loves you or whom you love is family. Co-workers, teammates, someone you share a bus with every day—these folks can be just as much a part of your family, potentially more so than even your ancestors.

We are all descended from the same progenitors. Our DNA started with someone—Adam if you like, or another member of Homo sapiens living in Africa. That someone then passed on his genes, along with those of the woman who bore his children, to the next generation. The story rolls on to the present day, and those initial genes, along with their mutations, remain within us all. A Shia is as genetically close to a Sunni as he is to another Shia. A Jew is only slightly less related to an Arab than she is to another Jew. An Indian and a Pakistani are just about genetically indistinguishable.

Here we have another clue, one which we could have explored in the first half of this book but which I have left until now because it so dramatic. We already know that each of us creates reality and that we each participate equally in the unfolding of the universe. But the existence and structure of our DNA affirms something else too. Not only do we all equally create the reality we experience, we are each a facet on the face of the same diamond. You and I are but minor variations on a universal theme. We six billion facets of this gem that is humanity each reflect light equally, each helping to create the vision that is our reality. We are enemies or family by *choice*.

Think about that for a moment. So many of us believe that our heritage, our religion, or even our family represents a connection that at least partially defines us and more critically separates us from those with whom no connection is obvious. These separations are more apparent than real. We are nearly identical to one another—our genetic codes differ only enough to make it interesting. This is not some wishful attempt at creating a brotherhood of man: there is a brotherhood of man! We differentiate and judge based on nonsense, as if there is some true and specific lineage for each of our cultures. Reflect on this: the earth is four billion years old. Mankind, in its present form, is probably only 100,000–200,000 years old. But our oldest ethnicities and religions are far younger than even that—even the most ancient ethnic and religious groups have existed for an almost immeasurably tiny fraction of the sum of man's time on Earth. We have built a myth on a foundation of artificial differences. We are all family, or at least we can choose to be family; our DNA and our eternal atoms support this statement.

If Mr. X treats his children poorly—if he cares little about their hopes and aspirations—then is he more "family" than Mrs. Y, their neighbor, who regularly dries the tears of the children when they scrape their knees in their yard? The Mrs. Y who makes them hot chocolate in the winter, throws a ball with them in the spring and celebrates the achievements that Mr. X ignores? She doesn't have as many genes in common with the kids—Mr. X has more. But the differences are slight.

Family in its most evolved form is love, and that love is independent of the genome from which it emanates. I have sixty employees for whom I am directly responsible. I love them, each of them. I want to know about each of their lives, I hurt when they hurt, and I celebrate with them when they have reason to do so. I care far more about the lives they can potentially lead than about whether they were perfect employees on any given day. I have decided that they are family.

Once again we can extrapolate. If family is defined as love, and love is unlimited, then our families can be enormous. Very few of us would take advantage of or intentionally injure a member of our family. So if we make our family enormous, then the chance that we will injure another is dramatically reduced. How large can our family be? Perhaps you are beginning to see where we are headed. There is no limit to the amount of currency we can accumulate when that currency is love. Therefore there is no limit to the size of our family. If our genes are nearly identical, and if love, the currency of life, is ubiquitous, then our family can be infinite in size. Infinite is a big number, and we really don't have to go quite that far. We can settle at around six billion or so, the total population of our earth in the early twenty-first century.

The story of DNA is a scientific tale of immense proportions. It is also the story of who we are—one family, with one common history. All of our divisions, all of our "separateness"—nationality, ethnicity, religion and even family—is just an illusion. When I watch a sporting event like the Olympics or the World Cup, I no longer root only for the Americans as I did when I was younger. Now I cheer for the best athlete to win, regardless of his or her nation of origin. Why, my children ask me, am I not rooting solely for my country? I love America, and I feel incredibly fortunate to live in the United States, where I can enjoy the freedom that is the privilege of all Americans. But I also recognize that there are no real boundaries or borders when we're talking about humanity. We are indeed one family. I celebrate the accomplishments of all people, no matter their nation of origin or their religion. In the next chapter I will describe the flip side of the same coin—sharing the pain of others as if it were your own (which it is).

We are but one family with a single origin. Once we accept this enormously powerful truth, we can begin to repair our world, just as a family heals its wounds.

chapter fourteen

VIOLENCE—

When will redemption come?
When we master the violence that fills our world.
When we look upon others as we would have them look upon us.
When we grant to every person the rights we claim for ourselves.

—FROM *The New Union Prayer Book*

Our illusory reality—the one we have created, the one that ignores many of the truths we have so far revealed in this book—confounds me. A short list of things which I did not "get" for many years would include: violence in any form, cruelty, brutality, child abuse, man's inhumanity to man (in whatever form it may take), racism, and bigotry. How could one man physically harm or kill another? How could someone intentionally injure a child? What makes someone act in such a manner?

Our world is full of contentiousness; we are constantly and literally at each other's throats. What are we to make of this? We have already discussed possible sources of this contentiousness. One, of course, is the concept that life is a zero-sum game, that your gain is my loss. Most people assume this to be true, and therefore their actions, while sometimes excessive, are not irrational. If you believe that you and your family—and by now I hope you can appreciate that it is not clear what "family" even means—must fight for your share of the pie, then it is only the degree of the fight that must be decided.

Sports have become—or maybe have always been—the metaphor for the zero-sum world. "Winning is everything" is the common cliché. Why? Because to the victors go the spoils: the fame, the fortune, the status, and the power. The losers get nothing. It's not just professional sports where this occurs. We witness this at all levels of sport, even in youth programs. Have we not all seen video of two dads in hand to hand combat at a ten-year-old's baseball game? Such escapades would not occur unless large numbers of people believed that winning is indeed absolutely critical for happiness in life.

Another possible explanation for our incredible capacity to inflict injury upon another must be that we don't actually appreciate the magnitude of the pain we inflict. Since I am a physician, I will employ a health care analogy to explain this phenomenon. Most Americans have some sort of health insurance. Although a co-pay is often required when we seek care and utilize our insurance, we are for the most part insulated from the real costs of the care we consume. We read about extremely high health care costs, but unless we are without insurance we never really feel the full weight of that financial burden. Sure, our premiums may go up annually, but this is relatively modest compared to the actual expenditures required, and very often our employers absorb at least some of this increase. We seek the care we need while remaining mostly oblivious to the real costs to businesses, government, and society.

Violence often has that same quality. Video games labeled "mature" are rife with unbelievable shootings, explosions, and general mayhem. Movies and television shows depict murders and mass killings as if they were nothing more than entertaining distractions. And guns are almost ubiquitous in the United States. Killing a man with a gun from a distance may sometimes seem more like a video game than what it actually is: the termination of a life and the incidental destruction of many more. It's so easy to do—how could it really mean anything? When we see a building blow up, learn of a homicide, or read about the mass murder of hundreds of women and children, we are often far removed from the actual pain. We need only turn the page, or flick a button on the remote to whisk ourselves to a beach or a beer commercial.

In the past, violence was far more personal. You punched or kicked another, struck him with a club or stone, or filleted him with a knife. Little distance existed between the victim and the perpetrator. Now we can murder hundreds or thousands from a great distance with the push of a single button. Humanity has become the cartoon character that pops up a bit sooty but otherwise fine after being blown to pieces by a stick of dynamite. We witness an incredibly violent event on the television and in the next breath someone is describing an exciting sporting event or celebrating the heat wave in January. Violence merges with images of easy living as if they were equivalent. We accept violence as part of our world because we have become immune to the pain it inflicts. It becomes hard to believe that something so pervasive can be as heinous as it seems.

What makes someone able to kill another? Taking a life is of no great import if life itself is felt to be of little value. For some on this earth—those who have never known love or kindness, those who have been born into and raised in an atmosphere of hatred and violence—life *is* of little value, so taking another's is of no concern. Chronically politically unstable African nations harbor groups who reflect this reality, but this is also sadly the case in much more developed areas of the world, including the United States. The vacuum created by the absence of love will most often be filled by the violence of hate.

There are of course those who embrace violence because they see it as nothing more than a mechanism to further a cause to which they are firmly committed. A terrorist believes that his God has told him to fight for of a rigid set of beliefs and actions and that serving God is the sole purpose of life. Failing to take the life of one who refuses to adhere to those beliefs would be the gravest sin, implying a disrespect for God's explicit instructions. To love God, such a person is convinced, is to obey what he believes to be God's orders, no matter the required actions.

The Hebrew Bible, the Old Testament, recounts the story of Abraham and Isaac (as does the Koran of Islam). God instructed Abraham to take his son Isaac up a mountain, bind him, and then slay him with a knife as a sacrifice to God. Abraham, the believer that he was, did as he was instructed, but just as he raised his knife-wielding hand to slay his son an angel appeared and stayed Abraham's hand. In God's name the angel praised Abraham, and God himself promised a brilliant future for Abraham's descendants because Abraham was willing to sacrifice his most precious possession, his son Isaac, to fulfill the will of God. Many learned scholars have analyzed and interpreted this story, and clearly it can mean many things to many people. Most accept this story as a metaphor. God demands much of us, but He is kind and compassionate and will reward us for our obedience.

Imagine if you thought you heard God tell you to take your child, tie him up, and slit his throat. Whether you followed through or merely recounted your holy orders doesn't matter: you would be deemed psychologically unstable, a threat to your family and society. Yet we read this story of a man who is ready to kill his child and we praise Abraham as a hero, a true believer, a great man of God. Most of us can do so because we read the sacrifice of Isaac as metaphor.

Unfortunately there are those who read Scripture not metaphorically but instead quite literally. Consider the case of the twenty-first century Islamic terrorist who understands the Koran to say that non-believers, non-Muslims, must either accept the Islamic version of the word of God or perish. Here we have a dilemma. Our terrorist is certain he is doing God's work. Life on Earth, he believes, is but temporary, so he has nothing to lose by following through on God's instructions. It is what comes next after this earthly life that counts, and to not follow the letter of the law as he understands it puts that most precious non-earthly existence at risk. It is not easy to interrupt that thought process. For a man such as this, killing another, even at the risk of losing his own life, may mean nothing more than a quicker path to the magnificence that he is certain will follow this earthly life. It is not possible to change his mind as long as the terrorist is convinced that the sole purpose of life is to fulfill the will of God and that his brand of faith, and it alone, reveals God's will. Only if we identify a different "will of God" can we hope to eliminate this particular type of violence.

If someone threatens you or someone you love, your natural instinct is often violent retaliation. The threat may be no more than a verbal insult, but some individuals may perceive this as a real threat because it is an attack on an otherwise fragile ego. When is violence reasonable? When is it appropriate? And what is "good" violence?

Good violence is an oxymoron. There is really no time that violence is warranted; there is no time when it is deserved or appropriate. All violence destroys. Even when it protects one life, it destroys another. Violence is debilitating for the individual and for all of humanity. Most of us know this in our hearts. We are aware that something is amiss, that something is out of balance when we feel violent or commit violence. We are never at peace with ourselves or with our world when we are violent. Surely though there are times when violence is acceptable, you might insist. Think of oppressive dictators and genocide. Isn't the threatened populace correct to defend themselves, to commit violence against the instigators?

It would seem so. When threatened or attacked and your very survival is at risk, who would deny the right of self-defense? Even our courts allow for this. Fight or flight: stay and fight violence with violence, or flee. Every fiber of our being encourages us to fight, to defend ourselves and our loved ones, to defend our beliefs, our land, and our institutions. Fighting for that which is most dear is not only defensible, we are taught, it is an imperative.

But that thinking holds only when we rely on our unexamined assumptions about life and the world—assumptions that have been proven incorrect and which serve only to buttress what is, in the end, an illusory worldview. If the purpose of life is survival, then of course any action that prolongs that survival is appropriate. But since longevity cannot be the goal of life—for all of the reasons we have already examined—then we should be willing to jettison our incorrect assumptions and rethink this issue.

Premature death might be the result of permitting violence to go unopposed. That's only a problem if death is to be avoided at all costs. Death is not what we typically imagine it to be. Since the death rate among humans is 100 percent, it's not as if resistance can change the outcome. It can only change the *timing* of the outcome. Without question permitting violence to occur without challenging it represents quite a risk: it involves sacrificing what we know—our lives, our time on this earth—for something completely unknown and possibly fictitious—whatever may follow this earthly existence. The risk, however, may not be as great as it seems, for three reasons. First, it is clear that our world is not what we think. Also, many clues strongly imply that death is also not what we think. And finally, life is finite no matter which path we choose. No single path or set of choices allows one to avoid death.

Still, life is all we have to hold on to. What comes next, if anything, is unknown. Life *is* valuable; it is not something to nonchalantly dismiss, and I am not suggesting that anyone do so. But the question we must answer is this: which is more critical, survival or refusing to be violent for any reason?

Violence is extremely personal, both to the victim and the victim's loved ones. But family, as we have explored in the past chapter, is far more extensive than we have assumed. I am personally sad for all of the death and destruction in our world. I am sad when I witness killing and suffering anywhere on this earth, whether in my neighborhood or on the other side of the planet. I am brought low when I see illness and hunger. I feel the emptiness of the lonely and forgotten. All of these things make me sad because the victims and the perpetrators are my family. They are also your family. Violence against anyone is violence against everyone.

So what do we do about violence? Is it an eye for any eye? Do we turn the other cheek? Which is it? What is "God's will?" Tomes have been written on these questions. Scripture has been analyzed over and over again in an attempt to divine the answers. "God, what do you wish me to do?" In reverence and in silence, billions of times every day around the world, this same question is asked. As we have already discussed, there are those who are certain of what God wishes. It is written plain as day, they will tell you, in the Christian Bible, in the Islamic Koran, in the Jewish Torah, in the Book of Mormon, or in some other religious text. But of course, the answers are not so clear. If they were, then the degree of contentiousness and violence in this world would be substantially reduced.

Maybe God wrote those books, maybe not. It's hard to imagine that he wrote them all—unless we are willing to accept that God has a poor memory or has changed his opinions from volume to volume. God, or whoever or whatever created all that there is, has given us something far more durable and analyzable than scrolls and books. He has given us the universe. He has given us the laws of physics and the genetic code, DNA. He has given us all of the clues we have already reviewed in this book, clues we will re-visit again in the next chapter. We don't need to argue over which interpretation of which religious text is correct. We don't need to fight about which should take precedence over another, or which holds the truth. God has given us something much more substantial and powerful: he has given us our world and our lives. These things tell the story. These things provide the answers.

In the next two chapters we will pull all of the clues together. We will be able to answer the question we posed in the first chapter and then asked repeatedly throughout this book: why are we here? The question of how to handle violence will become apparent. It will be easy, because the solution is right in front of our eyes. We have made life a mystery novel, when in fact it has always been simply a recipe book.

chapter fifteen

NOTHING BUT NOW

I have a friend with whom I work who remembers everything. In the early days of our friendship I would occasionally find myself arguing with her about whether a current situation had been previously discussed. "We never talked about that issue," I would argue. "No, we actually did, and this is what we decided," she would reply in her quiet manner, never raising her voice to further her point. She didn't need to; she was always right. Now when some bit of historical information is required, I simply turn to her, ask her what transpired, and assume her response is factually correct.

It's not just work-related issues that I have difficulty recalling. I have read a fair number of books—still do. If you were to hand me one that I had read a year or so ago, it is highly probable that I would not recall more than a few key ideas. The same is true for movies. After about thirty minutes spent watching a movie, sometimes I'm surprised to realize that I've seen it before. "Hey, I've seen this movie," I'll think. "I don't remember the plot, but I think I liked it." Events and names seem to leak out of my memory, so that when I try to recall some detail the search comes up dry.

For a long time I just assumed I had a problem, some defect in my memory banks. "Bad chip," I would mutter to myself. I came to accept this obvious weakness, though I remained jealous of those individuals, like my friend, who have steel-trap memories. Recently another idiosyncrasy of mine triggered a bout of reflection: I have never had an interest in accumulating stuff. My wife collects many items—glassware, china, Christmas ornaments, cookbooks—the list goes on for awhile.

I, on the other hand, collect nothing. Collectables of any kind, even those that most would recognize to be of significant historical value, hold no interest for me. Except for a small gift my father gave me when I was six, I possess nothing of my remote past. If I chose to do so, I could fabricate my entire childhood, since no artifact remains to prove my story one way or the other.

What is the relevance of my lack of memory and my disinterest in historical artifacts? To understand this, we must briefly revisit relativity. Recall that all of time—past, present, and future—is very much alive simultaneously. Time does not flow. What we really have are an infinite number of adjacent "nows." All moments have equivalent standing. Our instinct is to assume that as each moment passes it becomes "grayed-out," like an option on a computer program menu that is unavailable to choose. But we have seen in our previous discussion that this is completely incorrect. Moments don't disappear. While our senses compel us to believe that the preceding moment is "history," in fact it is no more so than the current moment.

As we discussed in chapter eight, each of us is required to act out our particular part, regardless of what has come before. Knowledge of history cannot halt the endless repetition of stereotypical human actions and the familiar events that they spawn. What counts is the current moment and what we choose to do in that moment, for it is the sum of every person's choices in the current moment that creates the active unfolding of the universe, what we call reality. No one moment is more significant to the universe than another; all moments are equivalent.

This sounds extreme; aren't some moments much more critical than others? The answer is no. There is no such thing as a "special moment" as far as the universe is concerned. Perhaps it is easier to accept this premise when you realize that what seems an insignificant or negative moment to you is assuredly a significant or jubilant moment for another person somewhere else on the planet. Your loved one dies; a child is born to someone else in a faraway place. Sorrow for you exists simultaneously with great joy for another. Your team lost the game, and you and your fellow fans are sad; the other team won, and its fans are ecstatic. At every instant, millions of us are experiencing something we consider special. The conclusion is unavoidable: all moments are special to someone. All moments are equivalent.

Once again, here is the quote from Deepak Chopra that I first shared in chapter ten: "There is only a single instant of time that keeps renewing itself over and over with infinite variety...In the one reality, the only time on the clock is now."

Living in the moment requires a certain detachment, a willingness to release the past as the next moment arrives. Living in the now also requires a certain attentiveness and an appreciation for the idea that every moment is important. I began this chapter with a discussion of my difficulty in recalling past events, even books and movies that I have read and seen. It eventually became clear that rather than viewing this as a personal failing, it could be interpreted as a mechanism for ensuring that I'm prepared for that next now. As Dr. Chopra writes, "It's only by letting go of each experience that you make room for the next." It is the current moment that is of greatest importance, but once that moment has occurred it becomes part of the past, replaced by the new now.

Since adolescence I have periodically and unintentionally asked myself an unusual question: "What is the furthest point of my life?" This query seems quite odd. First, what does "the furthest point of my life" mean? Wouldn't the exact moment that I pose the question by definition be the "furthest" moment of my life? Something else was implied by this question, something having to do more with significance than with chronological time. At a young age, I sensed that there was something strange about time. I harbored a notion that the linear progression of advancing time that we have assumed to be correct may in fact not be accurate. It failed to explain this feeling within me —that's what it was, a feeling—that the "furthest" point of my life was not in fact the same as the current moment.

My "furthest moment" issue reflects a truth about time and our world. Life is an infinite progression of moments, of nows. But rather than viewing a person's life as a linear sequence of moments, we can visualize that life as a whole, as a collection of all of that life's moments viewed simultaneously. One can pluck out single moments of that life in any order; they need not be placed in the order in which they seemingly occurred. My "furthest point" question reflected this sense that the current moment was only one of many moments. While it seemed to be the most recent—the "furthest" from my birth—this alone gave it no special significance. Our linear concept of time is an illusion, proven by Einstein and others.

Since our lives are finite, our total number of nows is also finite. Our individual lives are a collection of these nows. By the end of our lives, we will have accumulated a portfolio of nows. These nows include all sorts of experiences. And what colors those experiences is the true essence of any moment—the broad spectrum of emotions that make us human: joy, sadness, fear, and of course love. Each now provides an opportunity to experience one or more of these emotions, the sum total of which defines our lives. Each now is a chance to engage with another person, to share a moment with him or her. It could be a moment of compassion or a moment of assistance. It could be a moment that we share a smile or a laugh, or a moment that we share a tear.

We have seen throughout this book what the world is not. So, then, what is the world? It is a collection of nows. Now is what counts—in fact it is all that counts. It is the experience of now that defines a life. It is the understanding that each now brings the opportunity to create a new reality, hopefully a meaningful reality. If you were a selfish person a moment ago, you squandered that moment of your life. Your behavior mattered very much at the time it was exhibited—maybe to yourself, maybe to someone else—but once that previous now is over, what matters is the next moment, the new now. This is when you make the shift from the person you have been to the person you wish to be. This is when you recognize that you have been chasing the wrong dream, that you have been mistakenly climbing that illusory pyramid. Now is when you decide that the world is something else entirely than what you had assumed. Each and every now is a remarkable opportunity; each is a moment of creation. This process of creation in every new moment is not a metaphor. It is entirely real and accurate and it is immensely powerful. It is how the world works.

What then is the purpose of this apparent progression of nows? Why is the world so constructed that our observations and choices actually create reality? What is the answer to Mr. Buchwald's question, posed in chapter one—why are we here in the first place? Below is a review of the major clues we have discussed throughout this book. Taken together they paint a compelling picture of what this world is, and they provide a framework to draw the conclusions that we'll need to solve Mr. Buchwald's riddle.

Time does not flow

Our sense of time is false. Past, present, and future are a deception, as Einstein and others have proven. The order of moments we perceive as time passing is an illusion, something created to make sense of our existence. Those near death or with what we call dementia often re-experience their lives in random order. Such re-ordering of time is viewed as an aberration, but it is possible to entertain alternative explanations in light of what we have learned about the nature of time.

Observation creates reality

Quantum physics has proven that the future can determine the present (and the past.) The observation of an event can alter the outcome.

What we see and experience is but one possibility out of many

Quantum physics states that objects don't have definite locations, just the probability of being in a certain location. This concept of probability describes a world that is much less certain than we imagine.

Our world is quite specific

The percentage of oxygen in the air, the force of gravity, the temperature at which water freezes, and many more details of nature must be exactly as they are for life to exist. The fact that our world is so constructed is an enormous clue. Our world doesn't have to be this way; it is but one possibility. But it is this way, this precise, particular way.

Collectively, we do not learn from history

We make the same mistakes and demonstrate the same patterns of behavior that we have for centuries.

We constantly change—we age, and then we die

Once again, this need not occur. We are programmed for senescence, but our software could have been written differently so that our cells would never die.

Reality is generated when we make a choice

A left turn instead of a right turn will alter reality and rewrite history. This is how the world works.

Man can reverse entropy, the natural law that states that disorder triumphs over order

We have the power to win every time if we so choose. Mankind, taken as a whole, is effectively omnipotent.

Cycles are the way of the world

No one reigns forever, and no country dominates forever. The powerful are brought low, and the meek often rise. If life were a pyramid to climb, once the pinnacle was reached victory would be assured. It is not.

The idea of what constitutes family is far more complicated than we assume

We all have a common origin, and the software of life, DNA, barely differs among us. We are all related. Whom we deem family—where on our genealogical tree we draw the cut-off line—is completely arbitrary.

Death cannot be that big a deal

We are all well aware of our mortality; we know life will end one day. It is of course incredibly sad to lose a loved one. But death is the most valuable clue to uncovering the purpose of life.

There is no "right" or "best" life

Each of us equally and consistently creates reality. The universe unfolds as a result of every person's choices; we are all equal in this regard.

The currency of life is love

So much of what we have always assumed to be true about our world and our place within it is just flat-out wrong. We must jettison the standard assumptions that we have for so long taken as truth, and with them our erroneous sense of what our lives are all about. No one life is more "correct" than another. That means that whether you are President of the United States or a homeless person on the streets of Los Angeles, your impact on reality is the same. Just about all of us would assume that the President has a far greater influence. After all, he could order a nuclear war, causing the death of millions. What could that homeless person do that has nearly that impact? That thinking holds only when you assume that there is a preferred way for the universe to unfold. We have already proven that there are in fact no special moments and that there is no preferred way for the universe to unfold. While of course the death of millions is horrific—and I am not minimizing the impact on those affected—from the point of view of the universe it only exchanges one reality for another. Choices made by that homeless person do the same.

Future events affect the present. Time is relative to the speed of the observer and anything moving at the speed of light experiences no passage of time. These statements seem so very weird to those of us living within the apparent framework of the real world, the world we can touch and experience, the world where time seems the same for all and where we seemingly march along in a straight line from past to future. That is because our world is like a closed box within which the standard, accepted rules seem to apply. If we could view our world from outside the box, we would see that much more is going on than what is understood to be happening by those inside. We know that the speed of light is the universe's speed limit; nothing can go faster. This fact was a major impetus for Einstein's thought experiments. If we were to exceed the speed of light, time would do funny things. It would become clear that sorting events into the categories of past and future is merely an artificial way of organizing the moments that comprise time. The speed of light is a limit for a reason.

All of the soft clues similarly point to a certain weirdness regarding the world. We age for no apparent biological reason; our software could be different. Each of us is required to traverse the same terrain as those who came before, and we seem required to individually learn through experience the same simple concepts that our ancestors did. Our standard assumptions about life are off base. Incorrect assumptions result in incorrect conclusions. Our world is a mess for a reason, and that reason is that we have misinterpreted our world and therefore have been aiming at the wrong target.

Our poor aim is no small problem. It is responsible for most of the unhappiness, violence, brutality, and unpleasantness in the world. Here's the good news: the correct target is not only identifiable, it is reachable, and in the final chapter we will see just what we must do to get there.

The Dreams

Usually we didn't open the office on Saturdays, but Dr. Benjamin was leaving on Monday for a medical conference in California and would be gone for the week.

"Flu season, Robert. You'll have your hands full for sure. Let's see patients until noon this Saturday and see if we can't make a dent before I take off. Oh, and I got a call last night at home from Rachel Lawrence, Frieda Jefferson's granddaughter. According to Rachel, Frieda's not doing very well. I'm going to have her come in Saturday. Nice woman, Frieda, but not easy. She'll tie you up in knots for hours, a burden you don't need while I'm away.

What a great kid she is, that Rachel. You'd think she was forty years old the way she handles the responsibility she's got on her plate. At twenty-two it's not easy taking care of a mother with debilitating multiple sclerosis and a grandmother with Parkinson's disease and diabetes. When I hear complaints about today's young people I always think of Rachel. There are lots of Rachels out there, Robert. Give them a chance and they will rise to the occasion. We just haven't asked enough of them."

Dr Benjamin paused, and after a few seconds he looked me in the eye and said, "So Saturday it is," then turned and walked into an exam room.

It wasn't that Dr. Benjamin didn't trust me with his patients or his office. On the contrary, I don't think he ever worried for a moment about us when he was gone. Of course, Dr. Benjamin never worried about anything, ever.

"How is it that you manage not to worry?" I once asked my mentor.

"Now Robert, that's a silly question for you to ask, because you already know the answer. Will worry change a diagnosis? Will

177

worry alter my treatment? Will worry yield a different outcome? Will worry keep anyone from eventually dying one day?"

Somehow the words "death" or "dying" managed to find their way into just about every answer to any question I posed to him. Dr. Benjamin was not preoccupied with death. He had a great deal of respect for it, even an admiration. Whenever he spoke of death and dying, which was fairly often, it was as if he and death were old colleagues who shared a common history. It never seemed supernatural or strange to me. When Dr. Benjamin spoke, you always knew that whatever words he uttered came from somewhere deep, somewhere significant, so when he talked about death it seemed very natural.

Saturday morning arrived, and by eight o'clock the waiting room was full. Just as Dr. Benjamin had predicted, we were inundated with a sneezing and coughing mass of humanity. Three and a half hours and buckets of antibiotics later, we were finally able to take a breath. By eleven-thirty, we had seen and treated over twenty patients.

"Who's next?" I asked my nurse, Shelly.

"Dr. Benjamin is still in with Mrs. Jefferson. She's the last patient."

■ ■ ■

I took a moment and marveled at how efficient I had become at listening to and evaluating patients. Just a year ago it would have taken me all day to see these patients, and by the end I would have been short-tempered and exhausted. Now I never lose my cool with a patient. When I'm most stressed, I just imagine the little angel that Dr. Benjamin taught me to conjure at just such times.

It was late afternoon on a day during my first summer with Dr. Benjamin. I'd had a particularly difficult series of patients, and my last patient had been the most trying of the group. He was intent on taking every opportunity to confront me as the examination proceeded. No matter what I said or did, this gentleman was determined to make my life miserable. When we concluded the exam, I exited the room to complete my notes. Dr. Benjamin had just finished with his patient and was seated at the desk between the exam rooms.

"Robert, I couldn't help but notice that you seemed a bit brusque with Mr. Collins just now."

"I know, I'm sorry Dr. Benjamin. My last four patients have been so difficult, and I think I just ran out of mental steam."

"Well, I can understand. I run out of steam now and then, more often these days than I would like to admit. But Robert, I never lose my cool with a patient. And you can't either." Dr. Benjamin motioned to me to sit and join him.

"Patients don't really care if you've had a bad day. They don't care if your car didn't start this morning, or if you forgot to pay a bill. They don't care if a family member is ill or if you can still taste that taco you ate last night. What they expect is that you will be ready to listen to them, that you will figure out what is wrong with them, and that you will give them what they need to feel better. Once that's done, most people, to be polite, will be perfectly happy to ask you how you are. But their minds are already out the door and on their way back to their life that was temporarily interrupted by some physical complaint."

The phone rang. When the light stopped flashing, he returned his gaze to me.

"You signed up to be a physician, Robert. You are always expected to act like a grown-up. There are those patients, on the other hand, who are in some ways like young children. They expect the best from you and may very well not reciprocate and give the best of themselves. And that's fine. Because it's not an equal relationship. No matter how rude or unreasonable the patient may be, you are still required to perform at the highest level. I like to imagine a little angel seated on my left shoulder. When I walk into an exam room and find a grumpy or even hostile patient, I pause. And just before I make the mistake of becoming embroiled in a most unpleasant altercation, my little angel reminds me of the asymmetry of the situation. 'You are the grownup,' she whispers. 'Mrs. Smith is entitled to your best no matter how distasteful her words or demeanor. So just take a deep breath, put a smile on your face, and just turn her right around from hostility to gratitude.' You might wish to create your own angel, Robert, to catch you just before you're about to say something regrettable. Left or right shoulder should work equally well."

■ ■ ■

Freida Jefferson was giving Dr. Benjamin a hug. She had a big smile on her face, and when she saw me in the hallway she waved.

"Nice boy you have here, Dr. Benjamin. You keep working on him and just maybe one day I'll let him take care of me."

Dr. Benjamin gently turned her toward the door and reminded her to take her medicines and to be good to her terrific granddaughter, Rachel. As the door to the waiting room closed behind Mrs. Jefferson, Dr. Benjamin turned to me.

"Want to get some lunch, Robert? If you have some time, I have an interesting story for you."

"Sure," I quickly responded. By now, Dr. Benjamin knew I was a sucker for his stories, and lunch was just the vehicle to deliver the real meal. After we finished all of our paperwork, we wandered down the block to the local diner. Within a minute we were ensconced in a booth near the back door.

"Hi Docs!" Ricky waved us as he approached the table. "Not often I see you two here on Saturday. We got us an epidemic or something?" Ricky laughed as he handed us menus.

"Flu season," Dr. Benjamin answered. "Trying to keep our heads, and everyone else's, above water. Tuna for me today, and a cup of coffee. Thanks." Dr. Benjamin smiled and handed back his menu.

"What's the soup, today?" I asked.

"Vegetable, same as every Saturday." Ricky laughed again. "But you weekday boys wouldn't know that."

"That would be great. A bowl of soup and a grilled cheese sandwich. Thanks."

Ricky took my menu. Just as he was about to head off to the kitchen, Dr. Benjamin stopped him.

"Give us a few minutes before you put in our order, will you Ricky? That okay with you Robert? It will give me time to recount that story I promised."

I couldn't have cared less about the soup or the sandwich. It was Dr. Benjamin's story I coveted. "Of course, that would be great," I replied.

"Ready?" he inquired, his eyes fixed on mine as if judging whether I was prepared for the tale. He must have decided I was, so he began.

"We all dream, Robert. I'm not referring to our hopes and aspirations. Every night as we sleep, we dream, all of us. Some remember their dreams, others don't. Whether we recall them or not, they occur intermittently all night long. Do you remember your dreams, Robert?"

"Some. But even the ones I recall fade very quickly once I awaken in the morning."

"Dreams are fascinating, aren't they? We create an entire play with a full set, all of the props, intricate characters with impressive dialogue, and often a bizarre plot. Don't you marvel at their intricacy? The connections we make in dreams would be unimaginable in the waking state. No one has yet explained the origin of dreams, nor do we have any firm understanding of their relationship to our real lives. But there is no doubt that dreams are critically important, some much more than others."

Dr. Benjamin began.

■ ■ ■

"Mohammed!" called the Lord.
"Yes, Allah, I am listening," answered Mohammed.
"Moses!" called the Lord.
"I am here," responded Moses.
"Jesus!" called the Lord.
"Yes, Father," replied Jesus.
"What have you done today?"
"I have given the people of Israel your law, the commandments which you instructed me to deliver as I descended the mountain," replied Moses.

"I have transcribed the words you have spoken to me, great Allah. I have told the people what is acceptable to you and what is not, as you have instructed me," said Mohammed.

"Today I preached from the mount. Today I traveled the land and taught the people that we are all your children, that we must love each other as we love ourselves, and that You expect each of us to be our brother's keeper," answered Jesus.

"Tell me, then," the Lord said, "why is the world filled with hate? Why do I observe men slaying men, and even women and children, in fierce brutality? Why do I witness the powerful oppressing the timid? Why is justice distorted by selfishness and hubris? Why are there children who are hungry and terrified and without the comfort of unconditional love? Why doesn't each man love the other, no matter his tribe or nation, no matter the color of his skin or the language of his spoken words? Is man not fashioned in my image?"

"Man is imperfect," answered Jesus. "You are his God, perfect in every way, and he is merely mortal."

"We are weak, you are strong," replied Mohammed.

"I begged my people to listen, but they have lost their way," said Moses.

The Lord spoke again. "Have I erred so poorly in my judgment? I have chosen you three to carry my Word to the people. Shall I blame you for the chaos and inhumanity that everywhere thrives? Might I have chosen more able prophets? Or was my message unclear? Did I so disguise the purpose of human life that it is undecipherable? Why are my people in such disharmony? Have I not given them life filled with love and beauty? Are not the mountains tall enough, the water clear enough, the sky blue enough? Is the bond of friendship or the opportunity to share love between man and woman or parent and child insufficient to appreciate what this world provides?"

The Lord grew quiet. After some time, he continued.

"While you each live with Me in the eternal moment, for your peoples the seasons revolve and the days move on. For them, my Word comes as an echo from the distant past. They need to be reminded once more, for they seem blind to the obvious. Tell me Moses, Jesus, Mohammed, what shall I do?"

Mohammed spoke first. "Oh, Lord, it is not for us to say. We have recorded your Word as you commanded. That should suffice."

"But it has not, Mohammed," Jesus responded. "Our people fight, they raise armies and shed blood, and for what reason? They assume us at odds with one another."

"Are we not at odds?" Moses interjected. "It seems we are."

Mohammed turned to Moses. "Your people oppress us."

"Your people threaten us," answered Moses. "As have your people throughout our history," he added, looking directly at Jesus.

The Lord watched the discussion escalate, the voices rising in pitch and volume.

After a moment the Lord interceded.

"It is no wonder, then, that my world is in tatters. It is no surprise that men heap violence upon the world and upon each other. You three, my chosen three, are at each other's throats. If you do not understand, then how can I expect men and women to make sense of this world?"

The Lord paused.

"I have decided. There must be a new prophet. Tell me, what type of prophet should he be?"

"He must be so strong that all men will fear him!" cried Mohammed.

"He must have powers beyond those of mere mortals, as you gave unto me in order that I might confront Pharaoh, so that none will doubt his word," added Moses.

"He must be able to work miracles, so that the people will be swept up in his presence and will listen to his teachings," said Jesus.

The Lord listened to his prophets. He loved them, but he knew they were mistaken.

"I have tried that path and I have failed. Many listened, but many forgot. Why would the people respond differently to the same words? No, they would not, and surely we would have this conversation again one day. To repeat the same would be foolish and would most certainly fail.

"I sent you three to tell all of my people how to behave, how to treat one another, how to make a world worth living in, and look at the result. No, I cannot tell them again; they must learn for themselves. I have provided all the clues they will need, and now they must discover those clues. Only then will they know why I have given them life. Only then will they change their ways.

"Yes, I know what you three are thinking. My people, my children will need help to understand if they are to follow a new path. But even great and magical prophets have not succeeded, and will not succeed. I will bring a new prophet, but he will be different. He will not speak from mountaintops or carry tablets. He will not lead a nation in war, and he shall command no troops. He will be weak where you were strong. He will possess no magical powers, and he will heal no one. Look with me, now, and you shall see him."

■ ■ ■

Daniel awoke, startled and shaking at three o'clock in the morning. The dream had been so strange that he was compelled to get up and turn on all of the lights in the house, in order to create the illusion of day. In his dream, time was out of kilter. Events from his childhood were juxtaposed with scenes from only yesterday. Scene followed scene. Each included someone from Daniel's life, but that someone was always in the wrong setting. His grandfather, dead for twenty-five years, counseled him about the virus that had just crashed the computers in Daniel's office. In another scene Daniel was a young boy playing basketball in summer camp. His teammate was a teenage Uncle Steven, now seventy. Next Daniel was at his fifth birthday party. Dennis, his colleague at work, was serving birthday cake to Eve, Daniel's nine-year-old sister.

Dreams featuring family members and friends were nothing new for Daniel. These people frequently played bit parts in the night's dramas, and often they spoke to him. The difference tonight was that although these people were displaced from their time and place in Daniel's life, it all seemed so natural and real. Daniel's heart was pounding. He put on his coat and walked into the crisp November air, trying to decide if he was awake or still dreaming.

Daniel's dream turned out to be but the first of a series. The following night another powerful dream enveloped him. Daniel stood between two pitched armies, one clearly Muslim and one he thought might be Christian or Jewish; he wasn't sure. Swords were flying, blood was everywhere. He was powerless to stop them. Suddenly, Daniel felt the coolness of steel on his back. As the sword sliced through his flesh, he knew he was about to die. Tears streamed down his face, and he heard himself say, "Are you not all my children? Do I not weep for each and every one?" And then he awoke.

The third night brought yet another dream. Daniel was in a bank standing at the teller's window. "What can I do for you?" the teller asked.

"I'm not sure," Daniel replied. "What can I do?"

"You can make a deposit, or a withdrawal, or both."

"I think I want to do both. But I don't seem to have any money." Daniel stood confused, but the teller smiled.

"Of course you do," she said. "Hold out your right hand."

Daniel did as he was told. He watched his hand grow until it was enormous. As it grew, people began to appear within it. The longer he stared at his gigantic hand, the more people he saw, until people of all colors and from every nation and religion on Earth were represented. Many were laughing and some were jumping in obvious celebration. They began to sing, at first quietly, but soon there was a great crescendo as their voices merged into one. Daniel saw that all of these joyful faces were now smiling and staring directly at him, and they blew him kisses and called him God. And then once again he awoke.

After the third night, Daniel was certain that his dreams were not accidental. Never before in his life had he experienced dreams so real and so purposeful, and he was convinced that more dreams would come. Something was required of him, he felt, but what it was he didn't know. Daniel assumed that it would become clear in subsequent dreams. On the fourth night he went to bed with great anticipation.

But there was no dream. Daniel awoke the next morning, puzzled. Three more nights passed. Again, nothing, not a single dream.

It had been a week since Daniel's first dream. He could think of little else. Work had become a distraction from what he was certain was a life-altering moment; all he wanted was to decipher the meaning of his dreams. At lunch he decided to take a walk and get some air. Some young children were sitting with their teacher near a statue of Albert Einstein. This was Daniel's favorite statue in the city. In the sculptor's pose, Einstein was seated, with his right elbow resting on his knee and his right hand supporting his chin. Einstein was thinking, clearly contemplating something important.

The teacher spoke to the children, "Remember we talked about Albert Einstein yesterday in class? He was a great thinker. What do you guess he is thinking about here?" she asked.

A little girl raised her hand. "Maybe he's trying to figure out what he's supposed to do next."

"And what do you think he's supposed to do next?"

The girl did not hesitate. "Well, of course he's supposed to save the world."

Daniel froze. There could be no question. His dreams were his calling, and he knew without any reservation what he, Daniel, was supposed to do. He immediately returned to his office and called a local television station where his neighbor worked as a reporter. Daniel described for his friend the events of the past week and the content of his dreams.

"But what do they mean?" his neighbor asked him.

With a serene smile on his face and with a voice absent of doubt, Daniel answered, "It means that the time has come to change the world."

Soon Daniel's story was news on every television station, in every newspaper, and on hundreds of websites worldwide. Within days, Daniel began to receive messages from others across the globe who had experienced similar dreams in the days after Daniel's television interview. And so commenced a worldwide movement that began with but one dreamer.

■ ■ ■

I waited for Dr. Benjamin to continue.

"And?" I asked.

"And what?"

"What happened to the movement? Is this a true story?"

"We'll just have to wait and see, Robert."

And with that, lunch arrived.

chapter sixteen

PERFECTION

Some people are do-it-yourselfers. Trial and error and elbow grease usually suffice, and if they make an error, well, so be it. My wife is one of those people, and I have often been amazed not only at her high rate of success, but even more by her calm acceptance when things go awry. Whatever the challenge, she'll give it a go; no formal training required. But American culture has moved towards the other pole. We have become super-specialized. In fact, the degree of specialization has become so extreme that we very often feel the need to ask an expert before we proceed with any decision. Of course, there are times that an expert is required, such as when calculating the amount of concrete necessary to support a building. For the less exacting areas of life, asking an expert can be a bit more problematic. One can ask the wrong person the right question, or the right person the wrong question. Both increase the probability of failure.

In our pursuit of an "expert opinion" on how to live a life, we rely on conventional wisdom. Conventional wisdom is simply the shared opinion of a group of presumed authorities, those we assume to have the knowledge and experience required for the particular issue under consideration. But when it comes to the question of how to live the optimum life, conventional wisdom has failed us. It has failed us because it is an example of asking the right people the wrong question. We assume that we need to position ourselves to climb the pyramid of success, and so we seek advice as to how best accomplish that goal. We aren't looking for a total reconstruction of our lives or a major revision of our life view. Usually we assume that we just need to tweak a few areas. Maybe we need help with choosing a career, or improving our relationships at work or with friends or a love interest. These might be termed minor adjustments. So we ask the experts what minor adjustments are required to make our lives more successful.

Minor adjustments have not gotten the job done. Minor adjustments to our interpretation of life are insufficient; they will never yield a different outcome for us, neither individually nor collectively, than what we have historically experienced. The definition of insanity, it is said, is to repeat the same actions again and again and to expect a different outcome. Yet that is precisely the history of mankind.

It's quite a leap to move to another completely different paradigm. Huge shifts often imply huge risk. Huge risk is not something people embrace, even when the potential payoff is enormous. Humans loathe change and uncertainty. Considering how close we have come to destroying everything and everyone, the risk ratio has been inverted. Failing to entertain other paradigms has become the riskier path for humanity. Relying on the same assumptions that have produced the world in which we find ourselves ignores centuries of accumulated evidence, much of which we have addressed in the preceding pages. Wide-scale death and destruction once required careful planning and a concentrated effort by many. Now a few individuals can make it happen. Even an accident can bring unparalleled disaster down on our heads.

A good deal of what we have been doing as a species—what we are still doing— has not succeeded and is not currently succeeding in producing a world that can be embraced by all humanity. Look around. Is the world really much different than it was a millennium ago? So many remain hungry and homeless, filled with despair and hopelessness. Is violence any less rampant? Brutality and inhumanity are hardly in retreat. Remember our little girl who assumed that all people buttered both sides of their bread? It is likely that her children will assume the same. Those formative years not only determine many of our adult habits, but what we learn during those years—lessons far more serious than how bread is buttered—is incorporated into our social DNA. Violence, brutality and inhumanity will pass into the next generation, and the next, and the next, unless someone in that line of succession has the insight and interest to find another way. If we maintain the same assumptions about life from generation to generation, of course our behaviors will persist. Why would we anticipate anything else?

Only when we are ready to reinterpret the world will we have reason to permanently alter our behaviors and our path. The preceding fifteen chapters have made the case that our long-held assumptions about our world and our lives are grossly incorrect, and that many of the goals that we have assumed were most important in life (those things for which most of us strive: money, fame, power, and longevity) distract us from the proper target. We can add to that the ever-present assumption that God has instructed a specific group of people to oppress and even murder members of other groups that don't agree with the narrow and detailed instructions He has supposedly shared only with them. Not only is this completely fictitious, it is hubris taken to the highest level. The belief that the universe—or God—has marked a group of people or a specific person as unique and special is to ignore the clear fact of a shared reality, a reality that is co-created by every person and by every group of people. The good news is that those who encourage hate and violence are always vanquished and brought low. But before that moment comes, much suffering typically ensues.

Art Buchwald is no longer alive, but we are ready to answer the question he framed near his death, the question with which we began this odyssey. Why are we here in the first place? I believe that the case has been made that we are not here to get rich, to achieve great power, to live as long as we can, or to sow death and destruction in the name of God. We have also demonstrated, I believe convincingly, that our world is not just a random chemistry experiment, that there is indeed purpose and meaning. If none of the standard explanations for our raison d'être fit the facts, then what *is* the purpose of our lives?

We are here to learn—that is clear. Life is an opportunity for learning and experiencing. What is it we need to learn? For sure we need to learn love, for love is the currency of life. Without currency, there is no possibility of investment and no hope of a future return on that investment. So it is with a life. Without love to invest, the value of any life can not appreciate. Without love, there is no hope for personal growth and achievement. As we progress through the required stages of life, from child to adult, we are continually afforded the opportunity to acquire more of life's currency, love, which we can then further invest. It is analogous to the currency with which we are all familiar, money. When employed, we earn money. We can then utilize that earned money to buy what we need and want. Just as a dollar invested in the economy has a multiplier effect—it gets earned and spent over and over—the love we earn and then give to others creates a cascade of warmth and goodness.

We acquire more of life's currency, love, through the job of caring for others. Many paths are available to us to do so. We can aid the poor or ill, we can educate the uneducated, and we can assist a friend or a stranger through a difficult time. The opportunities are of course endless. All of these acts involve the creation and nurturing of interpersonal relationships. As we develop interpersonal relationships, our personal fortune—our accumulated asset of love—grows. We can then spend that abundance of love building even more relationships. *It is the development of interpersonal relationships that is the engine for personal wealth creation.*

When we think about relationships, we envision boyfriend and girlfriend, husband and wife, parent and child, close friendships, and so on. This definition is too narrow; relationships can be defined more broadly. Each and every interaction between two people is a relationship. You are seated at a restaurant, and the waitress comes to take your order. "So what would you like?" she asks. If your response includes only your choice of meal, you have missed an opportunity to not only create a relationship but also to direct the unfolding of the universe. Suppose instead of just giving her your order you respond, "Hi, what's your name?" Engagement of this kind can have unanticipated and significant repercussions. After she tells you her name, you might follow with another question about her life. The actual question is not important. You have humanized her; she is a fellow human being with a name and a history. Your recognition may be enough to put a smile on her face and lift her spirit, and perhaps the next customer is so impressed with her demeanor that he offers her an interview for a job that may change her life. Your simple act has led to a new reality for this young woman. This is not a Disney movie; this happens every moment of every day.

This broader definition of the word "relationship" is critical to understanding life's purpose. Physicians like me have the opportunity to connect to many people each day. Most patients come to see us because of a current physical problem or because they're concerned about acquiring an illness in the future. Patients are often vulnerable, and they see the physician as a safe and educated listener. Clergymen fill a similar role. Individuals seek out medical personnel and clergy members because it is accepted that it's their job to listen and to help. While these professionals have an obvious opportunity to engage the stranger, it is less obvious but no less true that all of us enjoy the same opportunity if we are willing to make ourselves available. It the responsibility of the electrician or the plumber, the office worker or the construction worker, the salesperson or the truck driver to do the same—to listen. All of us have a responsibility to listen to and assist others whether we know them (yet) or not. Many cultures place a high priority on kindness and hospitality towards strangers. These cultures understand the centrality of relationships in a meaningful life.

As you engage a stranger, you hone your ability to connect with others. The more people you engage, the greater your skill and your confidence for the next opportunity. Each connection is a potential relationship, and each new relationship advances your personal growth and earns you more of life's currency, love.

To further our answer to Mr. Buchwald's question, we need to return to the issue of God. Not only do we argue over the rules and regulations of our varied religions, we also disagree about the nature of God. Is God the anthropomorphic father figure that many assume him to be? Is God a more obscure and omniscient entity, formless but ever-present? Does God regulate our daily activities? Will our prayers determine the outcome of an illness, or procure good fortune for ourselves? Does God choose the winner of the Super Bowl or the World Cup? These questions have spawned endless debates, all of them unresolved. Regardless of what form God takes or what powers he is thought to have, God is assumed to be the creator. Even for those who don't believe in God, there is often an acceptance that some entity or force created the universe. The Big Bang theory states that everything in the universe began from an incredibly dense point of energy, often called the singularity. From this infinitesimal "dot" of energy, the entire universe sprang. The energy came from somewhere, so for many people (though admittedly not all) creation is a given, and therefore some type of creator—whatever its form—is as well.

What are humans? What are men, women, and children? Are we merely biological organisms that result from the genetic competition that is evolution? As we have seen, every decision and choice we make creates reality. We are therefore also creators, every one of us, and in that sense we all possess some portion of divine power. We cannot make the seas part or bring manna from heaven. We cannot raise the dead or turn water into chardonnay. The truth is that we really don't know if these events ever occurred. We can leave that to atheists and believers to argue. Since humans cannot perform those types of magical transformations, we may think of ourselves as immature deities. We come into the world with the power to create and therefore with some element of divinity.

"Hear O Israel, the Lord is our God, the Lord is One." This famous prayer from the Old Testament, the Jewish Torah, has long intrigued me. What does "The Lord is One" mean? Most commonly this verse is interpreted to signify that there is only one God. In light of what we have discussed in this book, however, a far different interpretation is possible. Humanity doesn't just share a common human ancestor: all the creatures of nature are descended from the first life form to arise on this planet. And, since the atoms that compose the universe have an ultimate, common origin as well, all life descends from the moment of creation itself. "The Lord is One" therefore can be interpreted as a statement of the unity of all that exists on this earth. "The Lord is One" means not that there is only one God, but that the one God is the sum of us all. Perhaps we haven't been able to "find" God because we have been looking for something outside of ourselves. We pray to the sky, to heaven, with the assumption that God is somewhere without, when in fact the Creator is within.

This of course is not an original idea; many others have proposed this interpretation. It gains more credibility, however, in light of the clues we have discussed. Each of us dies, yet nothing in the world changes. We are replaced, and the universe continues. Since each of us dies, since everything dies, death cannot be that big a deal. There is a changeless totality. Each of us is born and eventually leaves, but the stage—the universe—remains, ready to accept the next player. Fame, fortune, and power are meaningless in such a framework since they are fleeting and have no lasting impact. One person dies, another arrives, and a new chapter begins.

All of these clues begin to make much more sense when we understand the unity of the universe. Modern physics has proven that matter is energy. Einstein's famous equation, $E=mc^2$, shows this equivalence. What physicists have recently learned is not so much that matter can be converted to energy—it can; this is what happens in nuclear reactions—but that matter is energy in a different form. Everything on Earth, including us, is bundled energy. We are in fact made of the same stuff as light.

This fact, while true and fascinating, is insufficient for explaining human life and its purpose. Clearly we are more than light. The conversion of energy to matter confirms the undeniable connection of all humanity to the origin of the universe. It does not explain consciousness or our freedom to determine our path, our free will, and these are what distinguish mankind from the remaining energy and matter in the universe. Free will means free choice, and we know that it is this freedom to choose and to decide that generates our individual power to create reality. It is this ability to create that is divine; it is this power to create that implies immense responsibility. Our decisions and choices initiate an unending cascade of events that influence the lives of countless others. *Our failure to fulfill our divine responsibilities is responsible for the state of our world.*

Six billion people, six billion facets of the diamond that is humanity, compose a single family—in fact a single entity. We are, all of us, descended from the primordial point of energy from which the universe itself sprang. Once again I remind you that this is not philosophy; this is science. Alone among the inhabitants of this earth, we have the power of consciousness and the power of free will, and therefore the power of creation.

Consciousness and free will provide the answer to Mr. Buchwald's question of life's purpose. We are here to grow and advance. We begin as an immature deity, born with the power to create reality but without the wisdom to act in a divine manner. For the transition to occur from that immature deity to something much more substantial, wisdom is required. Life is a journey towards the accumulation of this required wisdom. It is an odyssey towards perfection, so that we can—at some time and in some manner—fulfill our divine responsibilities. To acquire this wisdom we must accumulate the currency of life—love. Our choices—how we exercise our free will—determine the course and the success or failure of our journey.

Without question we must learn to love each other, especially the stranger, if we are to reach our potential. Of course the stranger is in fact a distant relative who shares a common origin with you and everyone you already love. "Love your neighbor as thyself" carries new meaning when you realize that you and your neighbor are inseparable in this way. Learning to love and to care for others—while ignoring the arbitrary separation inherent in the concepts of religion, nationality, tribe, or even family—is necessary to reach our goal.

Death, supreme among all of the clues we have discussed, instructs us that our mission is to gain wisdom. This book was almost entitled, *If Abraham Lincoln Had Not Been Assassinated He Would Still Be Dead Now*. While it may have made for a bizarre title, nevertheless the statement is true. Everyone and everything passes from this life. If John Wilkes Booth and his co-conspirators—Lincoln's murderers—had never lived or had been killed during the Civil War, Lincoln would still not be around today. Even great accomplishments and great humanity cannot alter the final outcome of our lives. Does this mean that we should not strive for greatness like Mr. Lincoln? No, in fact we *must* strive for greatness. It is the striving that matters, not the outcome. It is through the striving, through our continued efforts, that we have the opportunity to fulfill our mission and to gain the required wisdom. The certainty of death reminds us that we need not be concerned about whether we live another year or decade. The number of years we have on this earth is irrelevant. Mr. Lincoln's life was cut short, but his legacy of justice and fairness survive. We must instead shift our focus away from survival to something else. That something else is the accumulation of wisdom. Wisdom is of little survival value; it comes too late. Wisdom is required for something far more important than longevity. *Wisdom is the prerequisite for perfected divinity.*

While we each are required to fulfill our individual responsibility to act out our unique role—as we have seen, this is unavoidable, and it explains the unceasing repetition of the stereotypic dramas in human life—we all share the act of creation. We have not recognized this very personal power of creation, and we certainly haven't recognized the additional proven truth that we are inseparable. Six billion immature deities act simultaneously, endlessly creating. Unfortunately, too often we act at cross-purposes because we don't recognize our common heritage and the ways in which we're connected to each other. Life's themes— creation, love, struggle, growth, and all the rest—are universal because we are six billion facets on the single diamond that is our world.

Since we are totally intertwined with one another—the actions of one affect the outcome for all—the well being of one affects the well being of all. If one of us is ill or in despair, we all are diminished. Some of us feel this most acutely, others less so. The chain is only as strong as its weakest link; humanity is only as strong as the weakest human. This explains not only why we have a sense of obligation to our fellow man, but also why we never feel quite right while injustice, poverty, and brutality persist. One of the survey questions in chapter three asked whether or not one of the primary goals of life was to perform as many kind acts as possible and to look out and care for each other. Eighty-nine percent of respondents agreed that indeed this was true. They came to that conclusion by looking to a truth that was deeply ingrained within them: all humanity is connected.

Violence is the hell we fear, and yet it is the hell we live. We create hell for each other right here on Earth, and we are quite accomplished at this task. But life is most definitely not a zero-sum game, and therefore the usual reasons given to harm or to kill or to destroy each other vanish. There is no possible argument to justify violence at any level. You may respond, "But sometimes violence is warranted, such as when I must protect myself and my family, or when I must protect my country." Without doubt, this is a most difficult concept to incorporate into our lives. How can any of us be expected to stand passively by while another, especially a loved one, is threatened? How do we answer that question?

Here is how: no one can take that which is most valuable from you, from your family, or from your country. What we assume we need and what we assume to be the valuable things in life—even good health and longevity—are in fact not the most precious. They are the illusions we have to come to accept as true because we have misunderstood life's purpose. Protecting ourselves and our families from harm or even death, while seemingly the most critical action we could ever perform, is not the most important. While I personally have a supremely hard time accepting this point, as I am certain most reading this will, and I cannot imagine allowing harm to come to my family, it is correct. Survival for ourselves personally or for our loved ones is not the point of life, since death is assured no matter what steps we take to avoid it. It seems an outrageous and preposterous statement. But all of the clues push us towards this conclusion. It is unsettling, but I am convinced that it is accurate.

Protecting even our children from death is impossible. But, you might counter, they should at least have the chance to live long lives, and so you insist that protecting them when they are still children is required. Of course living a long life is desirable, and of course doing what we can to provide safety and security to our children is important. But it is not mere existence that counts. What counts is whether that existence leads to the acquisition of love and wisdom. By all means, we should keep our children safe and love and nurture them. But if you protect your children and don't teach them that love is paramount and that violence is anathema, then you will have failed them. You will have missed the opportunity to advance the most critical aspect of their education.

Similarly, accumulating financial wealth and seeking power (with the goal of securing yourself and your family) are equally pointless pursuits. You can never secure yourself or your family; the universality and inevitability of death are the evidence. What you need to do is to acquire and spend love, and no one can keep you from this task. Violence is never appropriate, for it always subjugates love, and this can never be permitted to occur. As Deepak Chopra wrote, "Getting serious about bringing violence to an end means giving up a personal stake in the world."

Since there is no "best life" or "right life" to envy or to aspire to, we are free to concentrate on performing acts and following paths that result in the accrual of love and wisdom. You can't possibly go wrong if you sacrifice something for another. Anything that brings you love and wisdom is to be embraced, and nothing matches the opportunity to accumulate both as much as giving of yourself for another. Since the goal of life is to advance one's divinity, and since the acquisition of love—which then leads to the acquisition of wisdom—is essential for that process, we need to constantly identify opportunities that will result in the growth of our portfolio of love.

We perpetually strive to make more money and look for the next opportunity to advance our careers or improve our station in life. These things seem natural because so many of us have assumed that money and power are the currency of life. There is nothing wrong with seeking professional growth or earning more money, as long as they do not become the major focus of our efforts. Wealth and power can sometimes become distractions in our search for wisdom and the perfection of our divinity.

Once you accept this interpretation of life, no one can ever take advantage of you. Since what matters most is accruing wisdom—specifically the wisdom gained through universal love—how could anyone possibly do anything to diminish you or to obstruct you from reaching that goal? Anxiety also vanishes when you recognize this truth. What could you possibly be anxious about? Your death or that of a loved one? Inevitable. Loss of status or income? Irrelevant. As long as you stay focused on the goal of perfecting your divinity through the accumulation and distribution of love, you need not be anxious. Life will unfold regardless of what you do, and death will one day arrive. Death is only a problem if you have squandered your time on Earth.

We fear the unexpected. Why? The unexpected is also inevitable. Our plans are often foiled; this is as it must be. If our lives were to unfold according to our neat plans, we would never confront adversity or face the myriad challenges common to all. Our educations would be contracted, our advancement toward divinity frozen. The critical lesson—that the universe unfolds no matter what transpires—would be missed.

We're being beaten over the head with clues, clues about the way the world really works. The world is telling us, begging us, to pay attention. We have the collective ability to make the world as we see fit. Remember entropy, and how I stated that we have the power to defeat a primary law of nature? Together we can create any world we wish. Our problem has been that we have assumed that we are divided by religion or culture, by geography and by economic status. These divisions, all of them, are pure fiction. We have created these artificial separations. When we choose to ignore them we can create the world we all seek. As our survey from chapter three demonstrated, most of us are inwardly aware that this is not only desirable but also possible.

How do we begin to remake the world? Here's how:

(1) We must first recognize that we have misinterpreted our world: it is not what we have assumed it to be. Just as time is different than we have assumed, so too are those things we typically covet——money, power, and longevity. They are illusions and distractions.

(2) We must understand and accept that there is no right or best life. Every choice and decision equally creates reality; each and

every individual has an equal affect on the unfolding of the universe. No life is more important or more valuable than another.

(3) Life is most definitely not a zero-sum game. There is a limitless supply of what we need most——love.

(4) We must accept that we are all one family. To love thy neighbor as thyself is to recognize the single origin of all mankind and our inseparability.

(5) We must reorient our thinking to acknowledge that the real purpose of life is to perfect our divinity. We perfect our divinity through the acquisition of wisdom. Love is the source of that wisdom, and we must earn and share it.

(6) Relationships are the path to love, and we must strive to develop as many as we can. Giving to others is not simply morally proper; giving is commerce. When we give to others, we are bartering our time and concern in exchange for love, and eventually for wisdom.

We must eliminate violence at all levels. The universe speaks to us in a language of clues. The clues teach us that there is never an excuse for violence, and that violence diminishes, destroys, and prevents us from reaching our target.

Once we realize that we are not living in a zero-sum world, everything changes. Competition for resources vanishes. No longer is there any reason for selfishness; by developing relationships and giving to one another, we accumulate the true currency of life, love. We can toss aside all of the anxiety associated with competition, all of the anxiety tied to the need to climb the imaginary pyramid of life, and the fear of losing what we have erroneously deemed most important.

Why are we violent? Usually it is because we fear that someone will keep us from obtaining what we believe we need for ourselves or our family, or that someone is attempting to take something from us that we deem valuable. But no one can keep you from obtaining what you need to reach your goal of achieving wisdom and perfecting your divinity. That something is love, and it is ubiquitous. Your most valuable possession is your capacity to love and help others; this cannot be stolen from you.

We must collectively rise up and destroy the violence in ourselves and in our communities, in our nations and in our religions, in our tribes and in our families. Mankind is a single unit. We are bound to each other, six billion facets on the single diamond. Our constituent parts—the atoms that compose us—are not only interchangeable but share a common source. We began as one, we will end as one. When we are violent we are estranged, when we love we are one. Would anyone willfully refuse the feeling of love? Would anyone trade it for the chaos that violence introduces into our hearts? We know that violence is anathema to our hearts and souls, and that it must be eliminated from this earth. What we have not yet learned is that we have both the reason and the power to make it so. Not in a thousand years, not tomorrow. We have the power now, at this very instant.

Imagine, I asked when we began, what we could accomplish if we were all pulling in the same direction. There is every reason for us all to pull in the same direction since we are inextricably connected as one family, and that direction is straight up. As we lift each other, we move closer to perfecting our divinity, for surely perfecting our divinity is the purpose of life. To date we have expended far more energy in the attempt to live longer lives than we have spent in the effort to live better lives. It is time for us to focus on the latter.

It all comes together in the end—all of the physics, all of the clues, and the feeling that there is something more to life—if we are open to a new way of viewing our world. We pray for heaven, when in fact Earth is heaven in waiting. Former President John F. Kennedy was more correct than he might have known when he said, in his inaugural address, "God's work on Earth must surely be our own." We have divine power; we can make of our world whatever we wish.

Other questions remain to be addressed. If the acquisition of love and wisdom is the focus of life, then why go to school? Why work, and why work hard? Why invent? Why create art and music? Why bother to act out the mundane lives of mortals when what we are really trying to do is become divine?

Here are the answers to those absolutely legitimate questions. The world is the stage on which we learn to perfect our divinity. We don't exist in a vacuum; we can't pluck love and wisdom from thin air. Remember that we are each required to perform our parts and speak our lines no matter how many times those lines have been previously recited by the millions who have preceded us. It is through the living of a life that we encounter opportunities to learn love and wisdom. Hard work and a continuous attempt to make the most of the gifts we have been given are essential if we are to successfully advance towards perfecting our divinity, because it is through the individual steps involved in those activities that we gain the knowledge, the love, and eventually the wisdom required.

Truth is valueless to those who aggressively avoid the light and purposefully shield their eyes and ears. Neither I nor anyone else can open the minds of those who are intent on keeping themselves sequestered from new ideas. They may fear that some new information will appear, information so obviously true that it shakes their world to its foundation and demands that long and firmly held convictions be shed. Those are the convictions that keep us apart, that divide and separate us—by nationality or race or religion—and which damn us to a continued world of violence and disharmony. The rest of us must insist on moving forward. We must hope that each day more eyes and ears will be opened to embrace a new way, a way that raises love to the level it deserves.

What comes next, after our earthly life? Dr. Kubler-Ross told us that her extensive research led her to conclude that death is not what we think. We are here to learn love and to perfect our divinity, but for what purpose remains at least in part a mystery. That vision lies outside the box of our earthly reality. On Earth, the speed of light is a limit; perhaps it keeps us from exiting the box that is our consciousness and seeing what lies beyond.

Our vision of heaven has been crafted by centuries of religious thought and philosophic inquiry. Most people assume heaven to be a place of utopian respite. Heaven is depicted as a place free from hunger and turmoil, a place where we are freed from the physical ailments that burdened us on Earth. Heaven is the reward for the travails we have endured as mortals. Nothing will be required or expected of us; we have earned this eternal retirement.

Something is wrong with this theory of heaven. Consider the life of a would-be physician. During the early years of education, obtaining good grades is critical for gaining acceptance to a four-year college, and continued academic excellence is required for admittance to medical school. The four years of medical school are followed by internship and residency, adding another three to seven years of education. Can you imagine if, after all of that effort, that young doctor was not required to see even a single patient and instead was given a lifetime financial stipend and a house—even a car and a thank-you note—for all of his or her efforts during those years of formal education?

This physician scenario is analogous to assuming that heaven will require nothing of us, simply because we have fulfilled our earthy education. It would be foolish of me to be dogmatic, but I am sanguine that what lies beyond for each of us instead will involve great responsibility. Why else would we need to perfect our divinity? Why else are we required to invest so much effort in accruing wisdom? Once we have accumulated that wisdom, doesn't it make far more sense that we will be expected to utilize that wisdom and our learned divinity? I believe that we will have much to do as we move from this realm to the next— what comes after will not be the vacation we assume. Too much transpires on Earth, too much has been invested in our education to believe that the hereafter is simply a permanent vacation. It is far more probable that there will be much work to be done, and that this work will employ our divine training. Rather than allowing ourselves to be disappointed in such a prospect, we should see it as inspiring and uplifting. We will have much to offer, and the rewards are likely to be beyond our ability to express, now or then.

Humanity is not stuck. We have unlimited power to remake our world. Every new now represents an opportunity for renewal. A world free of violence, a world filled with love and compassion—this is what awaits us when we understand what our world is and why we are here. This world is the training ground for the divine, and we are the students. We need to abandon selfishness and violence, and we must instead work to perfect our ability to love and to gain the wisdom that will be required for whatever comes next. Teach this to your neighbor, and encourage him or her to do the same. One day, we will arrive at the ultimate now, that moment when all people on Earth will understand life's purpose. And when that light goes on, all six billion will simultaneously pull together, raising us all. Then the world will be healed, and even God will smile.

Index

A

Absurdity of life, 111–112
Accumulation of material possessions, 135
Acquiring love, 192–193
  loving strangers, 193, 196
Aging, 68–72
  death, 113–120
Anxiety, 199–200
Approaching the meaning of life, 27–36
Atheists, 133
Audacity of Hope, The, 132–133

B

Bees, 135
Benjamin, Dr. Jim, 3–5, 10, 97–98, 106, 177–181, 187
Big Bang theory, 194
Black swan events, 110
Black Swan, The, 110
Blessings, 97
Book of Secrets, 122
Buchwald, Art, 21–22

C

Camus, Albert, 111
Children, teaching about love, 198
Choices, 80–82, 136–138, 157
Chopra, Deepak, 121–123, 171, 199
Civilizations, demise of, 68
Clues to the meaning of life, 25, 35–36, 173–175, 200–201
  belief that doing good deeds is desirable, 33
  Deepak Chopra, 122–123
  entropy and disorder, 83–85
  fragility of life, 136
  hard clues
    quantum physics. *See* Quantum physics
    relativity. *See* Relativity
    lack of ability to predict future events, 110–111

  repetition of history, 88–90
  return of asset value to zero at death, 136
  soft clues, 36, 63–66
    aging, 68–72
    creationism and evolution, 66
    demise of civilizations, 68
    intelligence and learning, 72–75
    ontogeny recapitulates phylogeny, 67–68
    randomness of our world, 66
    randomness vs. purpose, 67
    repetition of history, 67–68
Concept of "now", 43
Consciousness, 123
Contemplation, 11–12
  God, and plight of humanity, 15–16
  meaning of life, 22–23
  misinterpretation of our world, 16
  self-dooming nature of man, 14–15
Contentiousness, 161–162
Conventional wisdom, 189
Creating reality, 77–81, 136–138, 172
Creationism, 66
Currency of life, 141–143
  existentialist philosophy, 143–144
  fame and fortune, 142–143, 148–149
  love, 146–149, 191
    acquiring, 192–193
    loving strangers, 193–196
  power, 146
  survival as meaning of life, 145
Current moment, 170–172
Cycles of life, 95, 174

D

da Vinci, Leonardo, 87
Darwin, Charles, 153
Death, 113
  Art Buchwald, 21–22
  fragility of life, 114–116
  inevitability of, 196
  Kubler-Ross, Elisabeth, 117–120

life after death, 204
moment of death, 117–118
nonexistence of death, 119–120
reconciling preciousness of life with
  irrelevance of life to universe, 116–
  117
return of asset value to zero, 136
survival as meaning of life, 145
Decision-making, 189–190
Discarding erroneous beliefs, 134–135
Disorder, 83–85
DNA, 155
  aging, 70
  families, 152–157
Double-slit experiment, 53–56
Dr. Seuss, 155
Dreams, 181, 184–187
Dumb moves, 72–73

E

E=mc², 195
Einstein, 125
Einstein, Albert, 39, 47, 59, 62, 119, 195
Entanglement, 59–62
Entropy, 83–85
Equilibrium, 82–83
Evolution, 66, 73, 90
  Darwin's theory of evolution, 153–154
  intelligence and human evolution,
  72–75
Existentialist philosophy, 19–20, 143–144
Expert opinions, 189–190

F

Fabric of the Cosmos, The, 37, 44
Fame and fortune, 142–143, 148–149
Family, 151–152
  choice of, 157
  DNA, 152–157
  size of, 158–159
Fragility of life, 114–116, 136
Free will, 135–136, 195
Freud, Sigmund, 109

G

Genetics. *See also* DNA
  families, 152–157
  the gene as the unit of evolution, 73
Goalpost analogy, 43
God
  creationism and evolution, 66
  definition of, 24
  gifts from, 167
  God's will, 166
  man plans, God laughs, 106–110
    absurdity of life, 111–112
    death, 113–116
    fragility of life, 114–116
    moment of death, 117–118
    nonexistence of death, 119–120
    predicting future events, 110–111
    reconciling preciousness of life
      with irrelevance of life to
      universe, 116–117
    serendipity of life, 112
  meaning of life, 24–25
  nature of, 193–195
  plight of humanity, 15–16
  religion, 133–134
  terrorism, 163–164, 191
Gödel, Kurt, 125
Greene, Brian, 37, 44, 47–48, 52

H

Happiness, 132
Hard clues to the meaning of life
  quantum physics, 51
    double-slit experiment, 53–56
    entanglement, 59–62
    impact of observation, 56, 58
    interference patterns, 52–54
    locality, 58–59
    probability versus certainty, 52
    waves, 52–54, 58
  relativity, 37–38
    concept of "now", 43
    length contraction, 41–42
    loaf of bread analogy, 47
    present moment, 45

"special" moments in time, 47, 170–171
speed of light, 40–41, 43–45, 48
time, 38–41
timelines, 45–46
Heaven, 203–204
Helping others, 32–33
Hesse, Herman, 20, 126
Historical artifacts, 170
History, 87–88
advancement of, 137–138
demise of civilizations, 68
repetition of, 67–68, 88–90
value of studying, 88–90
Honey bees, 135
Humanity
divine responsibilities, 195–197, 204
mundane aspects of life, 20–23
nature of, 13–15
origin of, 194

I

Infinity, 125
Intelligence, 72–75
Interference patterns, 52–54
Isaacson, Walter, 125

K

Kennedy, John F., 202
Kennedy, Robert, 137–138
Kubler-Ross, Elisabeth, 117–121, 124, 203

L

Learning, 72–75
Length contraction, 41–42
Life
absurdity of life, 111–112
as a zero-sum game, 132
currency of. *See* Currency of life
cycles of, 95, 174
death, 113–116
fragility of life, 114–116, 136
meaning of life. *See* Meaning of life
moment of death, 117–118
mundane aspects of life, 20–23

nonexistence of death, 119–120
reconciling preciousness of life with irrelevance of life to universe, 116–117
serendipity of life, 112
survival as meaning of life, 145
veneer of life, 122
Light waves, 52, 54
Lincoln, Abraham, 196–197
Living in the moment, 171
Loaf of bread analogy, 47
Locality, 58–59
Love, 146–149, 191
acquiring, 192–193
as the currency of life, 146–149, 191
loving strangers, 193, 196
sacrifice, 199
teaching children about, 198

M

Man plans, God laughs, 106–110
absurdity of life, 111–112
death, 113–116
fragility of life, 114–116
moment of death, 117–118
nonexistence of death, 119–120
predicting future events, 110–111
reconciling preciousness of life with irrelevance of life to universe, 116–117
serendipity of life, 112
Man. *See* Humanity
Mann, Thomas, 20
Meaning of life, 22–23
approaching the question, 27–36
clues. *See* Clues to the meaning of life
love. *See* Love
potential explanations, 24–25
survival as meaning of life, 145
wisdom, 196–197
Memory, 124–125, 169
Misinterpretation of our world, 16
Mistakes, repetition of, 72
Mundane aspects of life, 20–23

N

New Union Prayer Book, The, 161
Newton, Sir Isaac, 59
Newtonian physics, 59
"Now," concept of, 43
Nows, 171–172

O

Obama, Barack, 132–133
Observation, impact of, 56, 58
Ontogeny recapitulates phylogeny, 67–68

P

Perfection
    perfecting our divinity, 202–203, 205
    striving for greatness, 196–197
Personal responsibility, 137
Philosophy, 12, 19
    existentialism, 143–144
Physics
    Newtonian physics, 59
    quantum physics. *See* Quantum
        physics
Plans, 107–110
    absurdity of life, 111–112
    death, 113–116
    fragility of life, 114–116
    predicting future events, 110–111
    serendipity of life, 112
Power and wealth, 139, 146
Predicting future events, 110–111
Present moment, 45, 170–172
Probability
    versus certainty, 52
    waves, 58
Psychology, 19

Q

Quantum physics, 51
    double-slit experiment, 53–56
    entanglement, 59–62
    impact of observation, 56, 58
    interference patterns, 52–54
    light waves, 52, 54

locality, 58–59
    probability versus certainty, 52
    probability waves, 58
    waves, 53
Questionnaire on the meaning of life,
    28–36

R

Randomness
    of life, 112
    of our world, 66
    vs. purpose, 67
Reality, 63–66, 77–85, 136–138, 172
    choices, 80–82, 136–138
    creating, 77–81, 136–138, 172
    discarding erroneous beliefs, 134–135
    entropy and disorder, 83–85
    equilibrium, 82–83
    observing creates reality, 58
    preferred outcomes, 81
    veneer of life, 122
Relationships
    development of interpersonal rela-
        tionships, 192–193
    with strangers, 193, 196
Relativity, 37–38
    length contraction, 41–42
    subjectivity of time, 125–126
    time, 38–41
        concept of "now", 43, 125
        loaf of bread analogy, 47
        present moment, 45
        "special" moments in time, 47,
            170–171
        speed of light, 40–41, 43–45, 48
        time dilation, 39–41
        timelines, 45–46
Religion, 133–134
    God's will, 166
    heaven, 203–204
    terrorism, 163–164, 191
Remaking the world, 200–201
Repetition of history, 67–68, 88–90
Richard Dawkins,, 73
Russert, Tim, 115

S

Sacrifice, 199
Sartre, Jean Paul, 19–20, 143
Schindler, Albert, 114
Schindler's List, 114
Self-dooming nature of man, 14–15
Selfish Gene, The, 73
Serendipity of life, 112
Siddhartha, 126
Soft clues to the meaning of life, 36, 63–66
  aging, 68–72
  creationism and evolution, 66
  demise of civilizations, 68
  intelligence and learning, 72–75
  ontogeny recapitulates phylogeny, 67–68
  randomness of our world, 66
  randomness vs. purpose, 67
  repetition of history, 67–68
"Special" moments in time, 47, 170–171
Speed of light, 40–41, 43–45, 48
Strangers
  kindness to, 197
  relationships with, 193, 196
Striving for greatness, 196–197
Surowiecki, James, 27
Survey on the meaning of life, 28–36

T

Taleb, Nassim Nicholas, 110
Tannen, Deborah, 123–124
Terrorism, 163–164, 191
Time
  current moment, 170–172
  dilation, 39–41
  illusion of, 123–126
  infinity, 125
  life after death, 118
  living in the moment, 171
  subjectivity of, 125–126
Time, relativity of, 38–41
  concept of "now", 43, 125
  length contraction, 41–42
  loaf of bread analogy, 47

"special" moments in time, 47, 170–171
time dilation, 39–41
timelines, 45–46

U

Unity of the universe, 195

V

Violence, 161
  contentiousness, 161–162
  destroying violence, 202
  distance from inflicted pain, 162–163
  God's will, 166
  inappropriateness of, 164–165, 199
  permitting, 165
  personal nature of, 166
  reason for, 201
  self-defense, 198
  terrorism, 163–164, 191

W

Waves, 52
  light waves, 52–54
  probability waves, 58
Wealth and power, 139
What Do I Do Now? A Handbook for Life, 72
Wisdom, 196–197
Wisdom of Crowds, The, 27
World
  bizarre nature of, 131
  remaking, 200–201
Worry, 17